THRiVE IN THE COMING SHOCKS TO EDUCATION

BECOME A SHOCK ABSORBER

Copyright © 2024

All rights reserved. No part of this publication may be reproduced, distributed, or transmitted in any form or by any means, including photocopying, recording, or other electronic or mechanical methods, without the prior written permission of the publisher, except in the case of brief quotations embodied in critical reviews and certain other noncommercial uses permitted by copyright law.

Book Design by HMDPUBLISHING

CONTENTS

Preface **4**
Who This Guide is For 7
How to Use This Guide..............................8
Before We Get Started: Important Federal Funding
Terms and Abbreviations 9

Introduction **13**
**Prepare to Act: Four Shocks Are Coming.
Are You Ready?** **13**

01. Shock #1: The End of Current Federal Funding . . . 21
02. Shock #2: Declining Enrollment in K-12 41
03. Shock #3: Ongoing Inflation and
 Changes in the Labor Market...................59
04. Shock #4: An Economic Slowdown (Recession) . . . 86
05. Time to Strategize! 95

About the Authors **101**
Authors' Contact Information 105
References..106

PREFACE

Thrive in the Coming Shocks to Education, Become a Shock Absorber is a practical guide to building capacity in school leaders and their teams to respond to the intensely shifting dynamics of the post-COVID-19 (Coronavirus) education environment. Understanding, identifying, and building strategies to sustain and fortify programs that address the new realities and needs of the post-COVID-19 education system is an urgent and critical task for school leaders and policymakers.

In August of 2022, the research team at Edunomics (Roza et al., 2022) hosted a webinar called *The Financial Forecast Is In! School District Budgets Are Headed For A Wild Ride*. The team listed the four atypical shocks coming to the education market:

- The end of current federal funding
- Declining enrollment in K-12
- Ongoing inflation and changes in the labor market
- An economic slowdown (recession)

While we found the webinar had incredible information, it didn't include ideas for helping district leaders do anything about the coming challenges. We left the webinar feeling a little hopeless for students and educators, and that led to the idea for this guide. We want to turn our ideas, research, and experience into a guide to arm district leaders with the tools to transform districts into shock absorbers that thrive instead of barely survive the four extraordinary shocks that are coming.

We knew no single person could tackle these issues and create this guide alone. We needed one another to bring the richness of our collective experiences, skills, and knowledge to bear if we were going to succeed in creating a practical guide. The same is true for putting our suggestions into practice. So, we're asking educators to reach out near and far to their teams, colleagues, and communities. Share victories and frustrations. Build common knowledge. Stay resilient. Count the authors of this guide among those people sharing the struggle with you. Reach out to us, knowing that we can help. We want to help. We welcome opportunities to engage with practitioners, lawmakers, and policymakers. You're invited to email us at become.a.shock.absorber@gmail.com for our support.

The four major shocks coming to education will require leaders to make hard decisions. This guide is for those who have the courage to make the hard, likely unpopular, but very necessary decisions. This guide is not for leaders searching for instant return on investment but those focusing on making an important and lasting difference in the next several years and beyond.

Law and policymakers must join school leaders in becoming shock absorbers for their communities. This partnership begins with awareness of how the unprecedented challenges placed on schools impact student achievement. The goal of this guide is to help district leaders and other key decision makers better understand complex economic factors at play and be prepared to thrive in the coming shocks to education.

Together we can address post-COVID-19 challenges, such as

- Learning loss
- Educator retention and recruitment
- Tight budgets facing increasing costs
- The social-emotional well-being of students and educators

WHO THIS GUIDE IS FOR

This guide and the authors' ongoing work will help school, law, and policy leaders lessen the impact of the fiscal cliff coming our way in 2024 and navigate the dynamics predicted to negatively impact school systems over the next ten plus years. Those who will especially benefit from this guide and the accompanying workbook include:

- current and upcoming school leaders at all levels of the school system;
- school boards;
- school business and finance staff;
- law and policymakers; and
- graduate and doctoral students.

HOW TO USE THIS GUIDE

Thrive in the Coming Shocks to Education, Become a Shock Absorber will support school leaders and their teams as they navigate the unprecedented circumstances caused by the four extraordinary shocks which are predicted to make sustaining and fortifying current systems challenging over the next few years. Successfully navigating these challenges is critical to meeting the growing demands of learning loss and the social-emotional well-being of students and educators while confronting the other powerful shocks now facing education. Content, tools, and activities in this guide are intended to assist schools and policy leaders with a thorough view of opportunities and risks.

BEFORE WE GET STARTED: IMPORTANT FEDERAL FUNDING TERMS AND ABBREVIATIONS

Term/Acronym	Definition
ARPA: American Rescue Plan Act March 2021	The American Rescue Plan Act of 2021 (ARPA) is a federal law passed in March 2021 to provide direct relief to Americans and contain the fallout from the COVID-19 virus. It was the third and largest round of stimulus funds passed to address the COVID-19 pandemic.
ARRA: American Recovery & Reinvestment Act of 2009	The American Recovery & Reinvestment Act (ARRA) is a federal piece of legislation passed in 2009 aimed at bringing the country out of a recession. ARRA was passed alongside the EduJobs Act (funds for personnel) in the era of the Great Recession. It was the most extensive countercyclical fiscal intervention in the U.S. since FDR's New Deal. Public schools received $64B of ARRA dollars and EduJobs provided an additional $10 billion to enable local educational agencies to hire, retain, and rehire employees who provided school-level educational and related services for early childhood, elementary, and secondary education.

CARES: Coronavirus Aid, Relief, and Economic Security Act March 2020	The Coronavirus Aid, Relief, and Economic Security (CARES) Act (2020) and the Coronavirus Response and Consolidated Appropriations Act (2021) provided economic assistance for American workers, families, small businesses, and industries. The CARES Act was created to implement a variety of programs to address issues related to the onset of the COVID-19 pandemic. The Consolidated Appropriations Act continued many of these programs by adding new phases, new allocations, and new guidance to address issues related to the continuation of the COVID-19 pandemic.
COLA: Cost-of-Living Adjustment	Since 1975, Social Security's general benefit increases have been based on increases in the cost of living, as measured by the Consumer Price Index. Such increases are referred to as Cost-of-Living Adjustments, or COLAs.
CRRSA: Coronavirus Response and Relief Supplemental Appropriation	The Coronavirus Response and Relief Supplemental Appropriation (CRRSA–ESSER II), a component of the COVID-19-related Education Stabilization Fund, enabled the second round of funding for K–12 schools and the Governor's Emergency Education Relief GEER.
EduJobs Act	The EduJobs Act provided funding to schools to hire, retain, and rehire employees who provided school-level educational and related services for early childhood, elementary, and secondary education. These funds worked in tandem with the State Fiscal Stabilization Fund as part of ARRA.

ESF: Education Stabilization Fund	The United States Department of Education (USDOE) created an overarching COVID-19 pandemic funding package for education called the Education Stabilization Fund (ESF). The K–12 components comprising this funding package include the Elementary Secondary Schools Emergency Relief Fund (ESSER), Governor's Emergency Education Relief Fund (GEER), and Emergency Assistance to Non-Public Schools.
ESSER: Elementary & Secondary Schools Emergency Relief Fund	The USDOE awarded Elementary & Secondary Schools Emergency Relief Fund (ESSER) grants to state educational agencies (SEAs) to provide local educational agencies (LEAs), including charter schools that are LEAs, with emergency relief funds to address the impact COVID-19 has had and continues to have on elementary and secondary schools across the nation. ESSER Fund awards to SEAs are in the same proportion as each state received funds under Part A of Title I of the Elementary and Secondary Education Act of 1965, as amended, in fiscal year 2019.
EANS: Emergency Assistance to Non-Public Schools	The Emergency Assistance to Non-Public Schools (EANS) is the K–12 funding component of the Education Stabilization Fund COVID-19 funding package which targets assistance to non-public schools.
GEER: Governor's Emergency Education Relief	Under the Governor's Emergency Education Relief (GEER), established in the CARES Act and further funded under the CRRSA Act, the USDOE awarded grants to governors to provide LEAs, institutions of higher education, and other education-related entities with emergency support in response to the COVID-19 pandemic. GEER funds for an LEA are intended to support its ability to continue providing educational services to its students and support the LEA's ongoing functionality.

Great Recession of 2008–2009	The Great Recession of 2008 to 2009 was the worst economic downturn in the U.S. since the Great Depression of the 1930s. During the Great Recession, domestic product declined 4.3%, the unemployment rate doubled to more than 10%, home prices fell roughly 30%, and, at its worst point, the S&P 500 was down 57% from its highs.
IDEA: Individuals with Disabilities Education Act	The Individuals with Disabilities Education Act (IDEA) is a law that ensures the right to a free, appropriate public education is available to eligible children with disabilities throughout the nation and guarantees special education and related services for those children. The IDEA governs how states and public agencies provide early intervention, special education, and related services to more than 7.5 million (as of the school year 2020-21) eligible infants, toddlers, children, and youth with disabilities.
RTT: Race to the Top	Race to the Top (RTT) was an education reform initiative under the State Fiscal Stabilization Fund that offered states incentives to implement systemic changes to improve teaching and learning in their schools. The initiative focused on four key areas of reform: improving standards and assessments, turning around low-performing schools, supporting effective teachers and staff, and tracking the progress of students and teachers.
SFSF: State Fiscal Stabilization Fund	The State Fiscal Stabilization Fund (SFSF) was provided to states by the USDOE to stabilize state and local budgets by avoiding reductions in education and other essential public services.

INTRODUCTION
PREPARE TO ACT: FOUR SHOCKS ARE COMING. ARE YOU READY?

September 2024 will bring a tremendous shift in the education market. COVID-19 stimulus funds will end, leaving education agencies with a new fiscal reality. Marguerite Roza and her team at Edunomics Lab (2022) out of Georgetown University are raising the alarm not only about the beginning of the end of the ESSER stimulus dollars but also three additional "atypical" shocks in the road just ahead.

Knowing the actual date of a coming shock creates a critical window of opportunity for educators. It may not be possible to prevent the coming shocks, but if education leaders recognize the dangers and move quickly there is time to prepare, time to strategize, and time to become a shock absorber.

The End of Current Federal Funding

The dreaded term fiscal cliff has been used often in the past few years. Now it's just around the corner: The deadline for obligation of the $190 billion dollars allotted to the Elementary and Secondary Schools Emergency Relief (ESSER; Gentz, 2022) Fund requires that the funds must either be obligated (have a set plan for spending) by September 2024 or be returned to the federal government.

Timeline of the Elementary and Secondary School Emergency Relief Funds ([ESSER]; 2021)

Source: *Afterschool Alliance*

The Afterschool Alliance captures the federal timeline associated with ESSER funds in this pdf. For updated official deadlines and announcements, refer to the Office of Elementary & Secondary Education (2024) website.

The USDOE's recent decision to allow schools to apply for *late liquidation* (Timmons et al., n.d.), with the possibility to actually spend (liquidate) the dollars beyond the original liquidation deadline, gives a new and fresh view of these funds. Districts that apply and are approved can essentially use 2024 as a planning year and, as long as contracts are signed (funds are obligated) by September 30, 2024, then the approved districts have up to 14 months beyond the 120 days already available to liquidate funds.

Regardless of whether a district must meet the original or the extended liquidation deadline, the September 30, 2024 obligation deadline applies. In both cases, if education leaders act quickly, there is time to prepare, time to strategize, and time to become a shock absorber.

Districts were initially slow to spend down ESSER funds, but the pace of spending rates has increased. What remains to be seen is if districts can (or will) spend most or all of their funds. What may happen to returned funds, no one knows.

Although ESSER funds were left untouched during the 2023 federal debt ceiling deal, other federal agencies with unobligated funds had to return their funds before the spending deadlines. It is very unlikely the USDOE will redistribute unobligated ESSER funds as additional competitive or formulaic education grants. Regardless of what happens, the funds will no longer be available to the district to spend.

Many of the hard decisions that will have to be made in preparation for the end of ESSER fund availability in September 2024 are similar to those that had to be made back in 2009 when American Recovery and Reinvestment Act (ARRA) funds ended. Lessons from 2009 can equip education leaders to make the best possible decisions as ESSER funds stop. The looming funding cliff will have a great impact, but by using the benefits of schools' collective experiences and taking a look back at history, districts can serve students and educators well, even in the face of the coming challenges.

The end of ESSER funds is significant in itself, but after these federal dollars drop off in September 2024, three other shocks are coming to the education system and education finance.

Declining Student Enrollment in K–12

It is important to identify factors impacting local enrollment trends to mitigate the associated financial challenges. Factors leading to declining enrollment vary, but contributing factors include shifting demographics (such as decreased birth rates and increased numbers of families moving to the South), culture wars (such as mistrust over curriculum content and management of social issues), and school choice movements (such as charter schools and vouchers).

Headlines have shown how many districts, especially large urban districts, have seen a decline in enrollment. As an example, ***The 74*** (Jacobson, 2022) reports that "The Oakland Unified Public Schools offers a preview of what other districts with declining enrollment and birth rates will soon confront: the painful and unpopular decision to close schools. In February, the district, which saw a 5.6% enrollment decline compared to 2021, decided to close seven schools (Finney, 2022) over the next two years. Four others will merge or reduce grade levels" (Jacobson, 2022, The fiscal cliff & 'Armageddon' section, para. 2).

Regardless of why enrollment is declining, the decline will result in potential ongoing shocks to school budgets in the coming years.

Ongoing Inflation and Changes in the Labor Market

Districts are not immune to inflation, and neither are the companies that provide goods and services to the education market. With summer 2022 inflation reaching an all-time 40-year high of 9.1%, school systems must brace for this hit. For example, districts have been armed with COVID-19 relief funds which have allowed greater than the usual cost of living adjustments (COLA) and step pay increases over the last few years. This allowed districts to increase annual salary raises from 3%–5% to the 5–8% range.

Financial reward in the form of pay raises for educators and staff is not only merited, but it's also critical for a quality workforce in education. Increased rates of pay plus inflation increase the total bite to district budgets in the 2022–2024 school years and beyond.

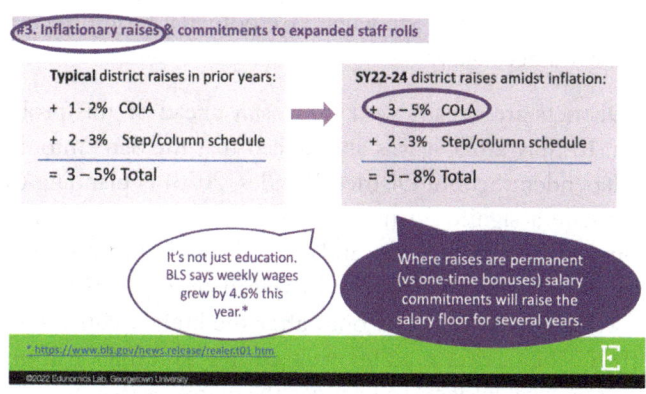

Source: https://edunomicslab.org/wp-content/uploads/2022/08/Perfect-storm-financial-forecast_8-18-22_webinar-slides.pdf
BLS = Bureau of Labor Statistics

Edunomics Lab provides a look at how inflation has increased both COLA percentages and teacher pay increases.

Transitioning from annual staff payment increases of 3%–5% to 5%–8% represents a substantial cost escalation. It's worth noting that the majority of a district's budget, approximately 85%, is allocated towards human capital expenses. The same is true for most business endeavors. To be sure, money spent on administrators, teachers, and other educators and staff is well spent and well deserved. But, given ongoing inflation, increased labor costs will have a great impact on budgets moving forward.

The expiration of stimulus funds now creates a real dilemma for districts. Each district must determine the best solutions for its circumstances in response to several key questions. Can the district sustain pay raises at current rates? If not, is there a risk of possible further blows to educator morale? Can expectations be successfully managed, allowing a return to lower percentages for pay raises without losing personnel? What other ways may there be to reduce overall operational costs without lowering rates of pay raises or negatively impacting students? Are potential hiring freezes or layoffs necessary?

Districts are already working to stay ahead of this problem. In May 2023, it was announced that the San Antonio Independent School District (Windes, 2023) is planning to eliminate a significant number of jobs—worth $22.5 million—in the central office and other departments to ensure that the effects of the larger raises given during the pandemic won't impact the classroom after the budget cuts are in effect. The district is additionally cutting $1.2 million from campus-level budgets to help pay the increases that have already been approved by the board. This will help them stay ahead of looming budget shortfalls for a year. Still, other drastic changes, such as contracts left unrenewed for hires made with stimulus funds and initiatives, are underway for SY 2024–2025.

An Economic Slowdown (Recession)

An economic slowdown impacts all areas of life. Business and industry are critical to drawing families into an area. If these areas are struggling, property taxes will struggle as well. This was evident in 2009 after the housing bubble, and will likely repeat in the coming years. A national recession will hit each state differently. A critical factor in how severely these shocks will affect school districts is the funding structure that a state utilizes.

For example, states that fund districts based on property taxes have fared better during hard economic times, while states that rely on sales tax, which depends on citizens choosing to spend their money, have a less stable mechanism. If individuals' purchase levels decrease, so do the state's tax coffers. This is not to say that school districts in states that rely on property tax are immune. The 2000s housing bubble was proof of that. Cooling real estate markets and more foreclosures mean less taxes to allocate for schools.

States differ on portion of district funds that come from the state

Reduced state revenues will hurt districts in states with greater reliance on state funding

Local funds tend to be driven by property taxes, which tend to be more stable in an economic downturn.

Within states, higher-poverty districts tend to be more reliant on state $ than more affluent districts

Source: National Center for Education Statistics (NCES), and Edunomics Lab

Edunomics Lab uses NCES data to provide a look at where reduced state revenues will have a more negative impact because of a state's larger reliance on state funding.

It is crucial for district leaders to have a comprehensive understanding of their unique circumstances regarding potential state funding impacts. Consider the dynamics in the local housing market and industries that play a pivotal role in supporting the district. For example, in Iowa, districts often fare better in recessions because their primary industry is insurance, which tends to be one of the last expenses consumers cut. Conversely, in Hawaii, districts rely heavily on tourism and leisure which are among the first areas of reduced spending during economic hard times. States like California, Washington, and Vermont that rely heavily on state funds will have to carefully consider how to navigate the coming recession.

# CHAPTER 1
SHOCK #1: THE END OF CURRENT FEDERAL FUNDING

ESSER funds are on a ticking clock. Come September 2024, the curtain falls on funds included in all districts' ESSER plans that have not been obligated (committed). Districts that did not apply and receive approval for the late liquidation option offered by the United States Department of Education (USDOE), must spend their funds by the original January 28, 2025 liquidation deadline. For districts approved for late liquidation, the final act plays out up to 14 months beyond the 120 days already available to liquidate funds.

The end of ESSER funds has been coming since the passage of the American Rescue Plan Act (ARPA) in March of 2021. In thinking about stimulus funds in response to the COVID-19 pandemic challenges, the key question is, "What did district leaders do the last time there were stimulus funds for education?" The last time education received stimulus money was for the American Recovery and Reinvestment Act (ARRA), passed in 2009 in response to the Great Recession of 2008-2009 and aimed at countering the job losses associated with that recession. Many of the challenges in 2009 were the same in 2021, and many outcomes were similar. This means it is wise to examine a few questions before getting to how to strategically spend ARPA dollars so ARPA outcomes are better than under ARRA.

ARRA 2009 vs. ARPA 2021: How do education leaders promote a robust recovery from a fiscal cliff?

Each time a new round of funding was announced, for many, the first thought was, this is too much, too fast (Gentz, 2023). It forced us to look back to ARRA and try to understand what was successful about it and why the federal government decided this was the best strategy when the COVID-19 pandemic hit.

The extent of a national economic slowdown will be unknown for some time, but history is on our side. Some of the key lessons learned from the last recession can be applied in the current situation. The following chart gives a high-level overview of the differences in leadership, funding mechanisms, and uses between the 2009 stimulus funds and the 2020 stimulus funds.

AARA/ARPA Comparison Chart		
	2009 American Recovery & Reinvestment Act (ARRA) in Response to the Great Recession 2009–2011 Funding Obligation Requirements	COVID-19 Funding Packages: Coronavirus Aid, Relief, and Economic Security Act (CARES, Coronavirus Response and Relief Supplemental Appropriation (CRSSA), American Rescue Plan Act (ARPA) 2020–2024 Funding Obligation Requirements
Presidential Administration	President Barack Obama	President Donald Trump
Purpose for Stimulus	The country was already in a recession when ARRA funds were allocated; districts needed to restore budget gaps from previous budget shortfalls.	Funds were needed to avert layoffs of teachers and other personnel. Further education reform in the key areas of teacher quality, standards, and assessments were a focus, as well as efforts to gather longitudinal data to improve instruction and strategies to support struggling schools.

Funding Rounds	One funding round	Three funding rounds
Components of Stimulus Packages	State Fiscal Stabilization Fund (SFSF), and the EduJobs Act (awarded 2009) Various components were geared to retain and hire educators; supplement Title I, Part A/IDEA funds; and provide school improvement grants for low-performing schools.	Education Stabilization Fund (awarded 2020–2022) K-12 component comprised of Elementary Secondary Schools Emergency Relief Fund (ESSER), Governor's Emergency Education Relief Fund (GEER), and Emergency Assistance to Non-Public Schools (EANS). Various components aimed at providing additional staff, technology for the purpose of reopening physical schools, and personal protective equipment (PPE). (These funds are separate from Title I, Part A.)
Amounts	Total K-12 funding: $64 billion SFSF–$54B EduJobs–$10B	Total K-12 funding: $190.5 billion Three funding allocations CARES–ESSER I–$13.5 billion CRSSA–ESSER II–$54.3 billion ARPA–ESSER III–$122.7 billion

Time to Obligate & Liquidate	Funded once over three state fiscal years, 2009–2011. Funds allocated under the SFSF and Title I, Part A/IDEA remained available for obligation until September 30, 2011, followed by a 90-day liquidation period.	Funded in three rounds over three years, 2021–2024. All funds must be obligated by September 30, 2024 and liquidated by January 28, 2025, unless approved by the USDOE for late liquidation, up to 14 months beyond the 120 days already available to liquidate funds.
Uses	Allowable use of funds was very directed. SFSF was used for district needs, but funding also went for school improvement grants, Race to the Top (RTT) funds were for education reform initiative efforts, and RTT assessments. The EduJobs component was specifically designed so districts could keep current staff paid and avoid layoffs.	Requirements for the first two funding rounds were very vague, requiring only that expenditures be related to needs arising from the pandemic. The market gave way to teacher shortages, not fear of layoffs. By round three of ARPA, there were some guidelines in place: at least 20% of funds must be used to address learning loss through evidence-based interventions that respond to students' academic, social, and emotional needs. The remaining funds can be used for any allowable use under the Elementary and Secondary Education Act; Individuals with Disabilities Education Act; Carl D. Perkins Career and Technical Education Act; and Adult Education and Family Literacy Act.

| Challenges | Ensuring that Recovery Act funds reached the intended recipients and achieved the desired results. In response to the recession rather than targeted directly for student success, funding was intended to help districts keep operating, retain staff, and avoid layoffs. | Emergency pandemic circumstances allowed no planning time and dramatically increased the mental health needs of students and staff, as well as necessary safety protocols. Fund expiration coincides with a recession, historical inflation, and significantly increased teacher shortages. It also comes before it is possible to address student learning loss caused by lost instructional time resulting from widespread school closures. |

In 2009, ARRA's total price tag was $840 billion, making it the largest countercyclical fiscal intervention in the U.S. since FDR's New Deal. Public schools received $64B of ARRA dollars.

Districts and states were allowed to use the money to restore cuts to K-12 and higher education to cover the cost of compensation and benefits for teachers and other employees. The funds could also be used for school modernization, renovation, and repair services.

Additionally, Congress enacted the EduJobs Act, which included funds specifically for personnel. EduJobs (Klein, 2020) provided an additional $10 billion to enable local educational agencies to hire, retain, or rehire employees who provided school-level educational and related services for early childhood, elementary, and secondary education. This was a separate funding source that helped to prevent layoffs for districts and is something American Rescue Plan Act (ARPA) funds do not include.

A stimulative fiscal policy involves lowering taxes, increasing financial transfers to individuals, increasing government purchases, or some combination of the three. (Financial transfers refer to payments made by the government for which no goods or services are exchanged. Transfer payments redistribute wealth by transferring money from one group to another.) The federal government pursued all three of these strategies as part of ARRA in 2009 and, to some extent, in COVID-19 stimulus rounds in 2020.

The ESSER funding included in ARPA differs slightly from ARRA/09. When ARRA was enacted, the economy was already in a recession. State revenues were falling, and the housing market was a large part of the problem—foreclosures impacted a great deal of revenue for school districts as many are funded by property taxes (82% in the 2016–2017 school year). States using sales tax also fared poorly as revenue from sales decreased in the recession.

It is important to look at the timing of when the federal stimulus funds were pumped into the economy, because it happened at two very different times. One was to boost the already recessionary economy, and the other was to prevent a recession.

The 2021 ARPA funding rounds during the pandemic came at a different point in the fiscal cycle. The markets were shaky and jumpy, but the recession had not started. ARPA funds came when spending was at an all-time high, causing supply shortages and shooting housing and car markets through the roof.

Another important context for the current round of stimulus is the current U.S. labor shortage.

The Center on Budget Policy Priorities (Stone, 2020, para. 3) states that "While the Great Recession measures were substantial and prevented an even more severe recession, they ended prematurely and were insufficient to promote a robust recovery." This was one of many lessons the Great Recession (ARRA era) provided. Well-intentioned ARRA funds did not adequately solve the issues because of the prolonged phase of elevated unemployment and underemployment following the economic contraction, which persisted even after the economy rebounded in June 2009.

Because the Coronavirus legislation has no provisions to automatically trigger further stimulus in response to worsening economic conditions, lawmakers need to be ready to implement policies that support work that started with stimulus funds. This preparation is unlikely, and means that a recession likely will not be avoided, and educators must be prepared for an economic slowdown and tightened budgets.

Admittedly, comparing the ARRA/2009 era to the ARPA/2021 era isn't comparing apples to apples because the context and timing of the stimulus funds were at different times and had two different end goals. But there are valuable lessons to be learned despite those differences.

The Institute for Education Sciences report, State, District and School Implementation of Reforms Promoted Under the Recovery Act 2009–2010 through 2011–2012 The Final Report From Charting the Progress of Education Reform: An Evaluation of the Recovery Act's Role (Trope et al., 2015), alerts us to several key takeaways from the ARRA stimulus funds. It's a good reminder that the goal of the funds was to make progress toward college-and-career-ready standards; create high-quality and reliable assessments for all students; establish pre-K to college and career data systems to foster environments of continuous improvement; make improvements in teacher effectiveness and help distribute qualified teachers in areas of most in need; and, provide effective interventions and support to lowest-performing schools.

How were the funds used?

Standards & Assessments

Embedded within the ARRA was the specific State Fiscal Stabilization Fund (SFSF). Education leaders used ARRA as a vehicle to directly fund SFSF education initiatives. As a condition for receipt of SFSF funds, the Recovery Act held states accountable for improving state academic standards and enhancing the quality of academic assessments. The final SFSF rules encouraged "states to work together to develop and implement common, internationally benchmarked standards and assessments aligned to those standards, to ensure that students are college-and-career ready" (Trope et al., 2015, p. xxii). This is where the Common Core State Standards, Smarter Balanced, and Partnership for Assessment of Readiness for College and Career (PARCC) assessments began. This was important because the governing law of the land was still No Child Left Behind, and, for all of its faults, the goal of education leaders was to be able to understand where their students fell in terms of academic achievement. Funding was allocated to encourage districts to adopt the new standards and assessments.

Ultimately, the standardized assessments had major impacts on teachers, requiring them to teach to the test. In the end, the policy was completely scrapped once the reauthorization happened in 2012 (Every Student Succeeds Act), making the use of funds on assessments an ineffective use of the stimulus funds.

Data Systems

Statewide longitudinal data systems had their day in the sun through the ARRA. Systems were to have 12 core components. $250 million was infused into the Statewide Longitudinal Data Systems (SLDS) grant program. ARRA also encouraged states to promote data use and access and included incentives for districts and schools to use the data. This was the federal government's attempt to increase the use of student data which could help inform and differentiate instruction and could also be used for school improvement grants at the lowest-performing schools. This increased the percentage of schools using student data to support instruction from 85% to 92%.

Educator & Workforce Development

States shortened or simplified educator licensure processes or authorized non-university preparation programs (which increased from 33 to 39 state education agencies (SEA)). Additionally, more states used guidelines for principal preparation programs (20 to 35 SEAs). ARRA incentivized tying student achievement to educator performance.

Improving Low-Achieving Schools

The Recovery Act continued the federal policy of identifying and providing resources to low-performing schools and also brought attention, substantial resources, and intensive reform requirements to the persistently lowest-achieving (PLA) schools. PLA schools are the state's lowest-achieving five percent of schools and secondary schools with chronically low graduation rates. The act provided an additional $3 billion for the Schools Improvement Grant (SIG) program.

This large infusion of funds came with new program requirements. In general, SEAs are required to (1) identify PLA schools, (2) competitively award SIG funds to districts that commit to implementing specific intervention models, and (3) provide technical assistance to districts and participating schools. The required intervention models—the transformation, restart, closure, and turnaround models—focus on significant changes to a school, such as leadership and staff changes, closure, or increased student learning time. Districts have the critical role of implementing the models and monitoring the progress of each SIG school.

Additionally, within ARRA was the Race to the Top (RTT) program. RTT also emphasized the focus on PLA schools, with roles for states to report on PLA schools or support districts implementing the school intervention models. RTT dollars were granted to districts that were working to implement performance-based evaluations for teachers and principals, adopting common standards, adopting policies that did not prohibit the expansion of high-quality charter schools, and turning around the lowest-performing schools and data systems.

To better understand context, governors across the country were trying to understand how their states were doing. No Child Left Behind opened the door for this environment. The goals were noble, but led to pushback from teachers and, ultimately, became political, especially when the Obama administration tied federal dollars to the implementation of common standards. After RTT dollars were introduced, the fund immediately became a Democrat initiative and began the battle for statewide standards and new assessments to stay alive.

One key takeaway from the ARRA report is that, among the indicators of reform that the study tracked, the prevalence and progress of reform implementation from 2009–2010 to 2011–2012 varied by indicator, or *assurance area* and level (state, district, or school). The report shows us that at the state level, 16 of the 18 indicators did report progress.

The assurance areas specifically included:

- making progress toward rigorous college-and-career ready standards and high-quality assessments that are valid and reliable for all students, including English language learners and students with disabilities;

- establishing pre-K to college and career data systems that track progress and foster continuous improvement;

- making improvements in teacher effectiveness and the equitable distribution of qualified teachers for all students, particularly students who are most in need; and

- providing intensive support and effective interventions to the lowest-performing schools.

While all assurance issues are still held to be admirable goals, the methods to reach the goals ultimately held us back as a country, and ultimately ended up squandering much of the ARRA dollars directed to education.

The idea behind ARRA was to spur innovation through the above-mentioned four assurance areas. It looked great on paper, but in practice, districts did not see the full benefit. This meant that districts were not focused as much on things like increasing student enrollment or concerns about inflation. They were also limited on actual innovation as the funds encouraged specific assurances. Instead, many districts used these funds to implement common core assessments that accompany assessment assurances, statewide longitudinal data systems, educator & workforce development, and school improvement grants—many of which showed little progress at the district. In fact, at the district level, only one assurance area showed increased activity. Across all levels, progress was seen most often in the standards and assessment reform indicators and least often for educator effectiveness and workforce development indicators.

Table ES-1. Top major challenge when implementing reforms, as reported by state education agencies (SEAs), districts, and schools, by assurance area: 2011-12

Assurance area and level		Challenge most frequently reported as major	Percent that reported challenge as a major challenge
Standards and assessments[1]	SEA	Lack of SEA staff or expertise to provide districts with professional development or technical assistance on developing interim or formative assessments to measure student mastery of the new or revised state content standards (16 of the 32 SEAs rated the challenge and perceived it as a major challenge)	50
	District	Insufficient funding to purchase new instructional materials aligned with new standards (95 percent of districts rated the challenge)	60
	School	Insufficient funding to support instructional specialists or coaches to help teachers implement new standards (84 percent of schools rated the challenge)	43
Data systems	SEA	Restrictions in rules and regulations on linking of student data to individual teachers (14 of the 42 SEAs rated the challenge and perceived it as a major challenge)	33
	District	Delays in transmission of assessment results to schools or teachers (94 percent of districts rated the challenge)	35
	School	Delays in transmission of assessment results to school or teachers (93 percent of schools rated the challenge)	21
Educator workforce development	SEA	Difficulty in measuring student growth for teachers in non-tested subjects (35 of the 46 SEAs rated the challenge and perceived it as a major challenge)	76
	District	Insufficient funding to provide differential compensation for teachers in high-need areas (e.g., low- performing schools, science, technology, engineering, and mathematics subjects) (53 percent of districts rated the challenge)	84
	School	Insufficient funding to provide performance-based compensation to all eligible teachers (49 percent of schools rated the challenge)	73
Improving low-performing schools	SEA	Restrictions in rules and regulations regarding the extent of autonomy that LEAs and schools can be granted in terms of staffing or budgets (15 of 49 SEAs rated the challenge and perceived it as a major challenge)	31
	District[2]	Insufficient funding to implement whole-school or turn around intervention models (65 percent of districts rated the challenge)	65
	School[3]	Restrictions in rules and regulations on replacing less effective teachers (76 percent of schools rated the challenge)	49

Source: State, District, and School Implementation of Reforms Promoted Under the Recovery Act: 2009-10 through 2011-12 (NCEE 20154016). Washington, DC: National Center for Education Evaluation and Regional Assistance, Institute of Education Sciences, U.S. Department of Education by Troppe, P., Milanowski, A., Garrison-Mogren, R., Webber, A., Gutmann, B., Reisner, E. and Goertz, M.

Nine days before the ARRA grant period ended, the USDOE offered states a waiver to extend the grant period for the Recovery Act Title I and other grants for an additional year so that districts could spend the remaining funds. The USDOE intentionally offered the waiver late in the grant period because it had previously encouraged districts to carefully plan for the appropriate and timely use of the funds. However, if the waiver had been available earlier, districts would have had more time to implement their plans or develop new plans for using the remaining Recovery Act Title I funds.

The USDOE could not offer a similar waiver for Recovery Act IDEA funds because the IDEA did not allow waivers to extend the grant period. Consequently, districts forfeited those funds not spent by the end of the grant period.

Lessons Learned from ARRA

There are clear lessons to be learned from the ARRA 2009 era, even though the variables for the economic and education climate are different now under the ARPA era. Among those lessons is a cautionary tale about failing to spend the federal dollars received by the deadline: the USDOE returned $6.3 billion, the second-highest return out of all 16 federal agencies. ESSER funds must be spent effectively and efficiently to avoid a return such as this.

Additionally, looking back at history gives us time to reflect on the long-term impact these funds had. For several years, Common Core and statewide assessments dominated the education landscape both in policy and in practice. RTT dollars helped ensure that states adopted both of these ideas. Once RTT dollars ran out—and fueled by some political backlash—state assessments and standards fizzled out in national discourse.

Among the priorities within ARRA funds, the only one that seems to remain and is still seen as useful in education is the state longitudinal data systems. In this time of stimulus funding, it is critical to consider which investments will have the greatest impact long term. Current investment trends are not as important as those that will still reap the benefits of investments in 5–10 years.

ARPA Plans Pivot

Major shifts are happening now in states' original plans for ESSER dollars provided through ARPA. Many districts have amended their previous plans based on lessons learned to date and to adjust to changes in the market and district needs. While some school leaders may not have thought about the need to alter details in their local plans, it is a very important consideration.

Regarding changes to states' plans, Burbio School Tracker 3/20: Changes in Virginia (Roche, 2023) shares some interesting points. "In Virginia, this education policy announcement from Governor Youngkin's office from October 2023 includes seven "action" points, the last of which is to, "Challenge each local school division to spend their remaining nearly $2 billion of federal Elementary and Secondary School Emergency Relief (ESSER) funds on proven efforts to recover learning…" (Governor of Virginia, n.d.). The Burbio report is cited in several revised ESSER III plans now being published in the first fiscal quarter in Virginia. Some examples that can be used as guidelines are shown below, with estimated ESSER III allocation in parenthesis (Roche, 2023).

- Norfolk Public Schools ("ARP ESSER III," 2022)
    - $27MM across strategies for tutoring

- $3.6MM for smartboards and a data management systems
- $60MM of HVAC-related spending
- Spotsylvania County Public Schools ("ESSER Funding Overview, 2022")
  - $1.5MM elimination in air-quality-related initiatives
  - $700,000 of professional learning initiatives, 20 full-time equivalent staffers
  - $10MM in tutoring-related programs
- Accomack County Public Schools ($13.4MM; "Updated ESSER III," 2022)
  - $1.6MM reduction of stipends for summer and afterschool programs at the elementary level
  - $167,000 eliminated for new buses for bookmobiles
  - $1MM increase on a Saturday Success Academy for Grades 3–5, middle school, and high school
  - $600,000 in reading programs for K–3
- Augusta County Public Schools ($10MM; Bond, 2021)
  - $1.5MM increase to $2.6MM on HVAC
  - $100,000 on mobile classrooms, $2.1MM reduction in building upgrades
  - $1.2MM increase in staff supplemental payments

Other states are also making adjustments in ESSER plans. In the three examples below, some common characteristics of plan changes include the following:

- Reduction of outdoor capital expenditures
- Adjustments and balancing of staffing requirements based on what is required to deliver services

- Reallocation of expenses from broader categories to more specific programs and tactics

Cartwright Elementary School District, AZ ($74.5MM; "Cartwright Elementary," 2023) is an unusual example of a district with a large number of material changes from their original ESSER plan, including:

- $4.4MM facilities project elimination
- $4.5MM elimination in field improvements
- $800,000 elimination in mitigation expenses
- $200,000 increase on face masks
- $3.8MM decrease in teaching staff $10MM increase in intervention and learning specialists
- $800,000 elimination in budgeted staff

KIPP Delta Public Schools, AR ($16.9MM; "American Rescue Plan," 2022) changes included:

- $1MM elimination of transportation expenses
- $1.8MM increase to $3.3MM in staffing pay and
- $342K increase to $1.3MM for additional bonus pay
- $500K increase to help target resources and support
- $240K to $430K increase for tutoring
- $375K to $570K increase for summer school

Woodland Joint Unified School District, CA (18MM; "ESSER III Expenditure," 2021) changes included:

- $1MM to $1.4MM increase for summer school
- $1.74MM to $1.47MM reduction for a virtual academy
- $1.9MM to $3.3MM increase for air filtration

- $2.5MM to $1.1MM decrease for paraprofessional support
- $972K to $320K decrease for library media staff
- $865,000 to $468,000 decrease for mental health services expansion
- $150,000 increase for COVID contact tracing
- $300,000 increase for supporting students in quarantine.

Edsource (Jones, 2022) highlighted several specific districts in California that reported improvements. Many others are working to decrease learning gaps.

- Mountain Valley Unified (n.d.), "a diverse, predominantly low-income K–12 district in the remote mountains of Trinity County, had some of the state's largest increases: 13 points in reading and 17 points in math, with overall results far above the state average" (Jones, 2022, para. 2). The district's learning loss plan included the following:
  - Later bus run schedules for students who need to stay after school to receive interventions to reach grade-level standards
  - A tutoring program for students in one-on-one or small group settings to target skills missed during lost instructional time
  - High-quality online intervention programs
  - Common Core project-based science, technology, engineering, and math (STEM) curriculum and tools to develop projects in the science and technology fields

- Common Core hands-on curriculum to provide students with enrichment activities that support the core curriculum in the humanities

• Lost Hills Union Elementary District (n.d.), "amid the pistachio and almond orchards northwest of Bakersfield, saw reading and math scores jump 12 and 17 points, respectively" (Jones, 2022, para. 3). An overview of the district's ESSER plan includes the following:

- Assessments to prioritize reading instruction, particularly for younger students
- Small groups established by the Acadience Assessment results for reading intervention
- Similar system established for math
- Short, progress-monitoring assessments taken once per week
- Continued quarterly benchmarks focusing on key standards
- Teacher responsibility for adapting core instruction or providing supplemental support if student performance falls in the "Standard Nearly Met" or "Standard Not Met" category

• Eastern Sierra Unified (n.d.), "a K–12 district in Mono County, also saw significant improvements. Math scores rose more than six points, with 32% of eighth graders scoring at the highest level" (Jones, 2022, para. 3). The district used a number of strategies in its use of ESSER funds, including:

- An increase in the number of instructional aids. The aids are primarily staffed at the elementary school site. The effectiveness of their impact on academic progress is measured through six-week cycle reviews where teachers and specialists review individual student progress on class performance and assessment achievement. Depending on student need, tiered intervention is assigned, and instructional aide staff is moved to respond to classrooms or assignments that are in the greatest need of student support.

- Student participation in a learning inventory and social-emotional learning (SEL) survey every three weeks. All data is collected and reported into a digital assessment tool in order to provide data on the growth and progress of students and the program.

It can be challenging to identify which states and districts are having success with the use of their funds. In addition to the examples shared here, search online for positive outcomes on NAEP exams or other assessments and then look at the district ESSER spending plan to see how much and where dollars were allocated to achieve positive outcomes using these funds.

Key Takeaways

In this chapter we discussed the importance of looking at history to inform our future decisions. We also discussed the importance of schools acting now to ensure effective use of ESSER funds by the deadline. Additionally, for districts that apply and are approved, the new timeline and allowance of late liquidation gives extra time to consider spending options before funds must be out the door, or liquidated. This also means there is additional time to switch up original ESSER plans to try and get the biggest return on investment out of the remaining ESSER funds. Head over to the *Thrive in the Coming Shocks to Education, Become a Shock Absorber Workbook* (aka *the workbook*) to dig into the themes in this chapter with your team!

CHAPTER 2
SHOCK #2: DECLINING ENROLLMENT IN K-12

Declining enrollment is both a short-term and a long-term problem. Not all communities are experiencing an enrollment decline currently, but over the next several years, all districts are expected to feel the impact of the "demographic bubble" effect described in Rice University, Kinder Institute's February 2023 article by Matt Dulin. According to Rice, urban districts are already seeing its effects, such as large budget cuts and educator shortages.

Depending on which part of the country you are in, it may not be obvious what all the fuss is about regarding declining enrollment. After all, most news reports on the subject are coming from national sources and highlighting larger school districts. However, as shown in the map below, states across the nation are seeing declines from students who did not return to public schools when schools reopened in 2022, with the exception of just a few states colored in gray and blue.

Public school enrollment declines since 2020

U.S. states public school enrollment declines by percentage, 2020-2022

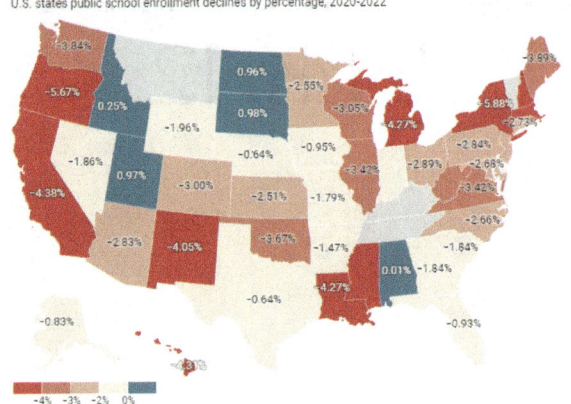

No data reported by Montana, Kentucky, Tennessee or Vermont
Map: @illinoispolicy · Source: ReturN2Learn Tracker · Created with Datawrapper

Source: ReturN2Learn

ReturN2Learn ("Chronic Absenteeism," 2023; Schmid, 2022) shows percentage of enrollment declines from SY 2020-2022.

Looking into the future, the impact of declining enrollment will exponentially increase. In addition to many students who did not return to the classroom, births in the United States are shrinking. Additionally, by 2050, the makeup of the U.S. population is predicted to change, causing notable demographic shifts in many areas across the country.

School leaders not yet affected should still ensure they are aware of Shock #2.

In February 2023, Texas Education Commissioner Mike Morath testified before the Texas State Senate Finance Committee, stating that Texas is entering a new demographic era of declining public school enrollment after years of booming new student enrollments related to growth within the state. The commissioner explained that Texas experienced a sharp decline (Dulin, 2023; Warren, 2023) after COVID-19, but a longer-term shift is occurring because of a 'demographic bubble' caused by declining birth rates due to the Great Recession of 2011. Moreover, net international immigration is down over the past 10 years. Though an individual district here or there may still be seeing robust growth, on the whole, all regions of Texas are expected to see the same decrease. As a result, enrollment is anticipated to fall about 2% over the next several years.

This is a somewhat more optimistic scenario than public school enrollment nationally, which is expected to fall 6% by 2030, according to federal estimates. The National Center for Education Statistics (NCES) forecasting bears this out, anticipating a decline of around two million students enrolled in American public schools through 2030.

In the chart shown below, Texas Education Agency data shows enrollment is down from Early Education to 7th grade in 2020–2021. Pre-K enrollment is down a whopping 50,000 enrollments while high school grade levels, except for 9th grade, increased.

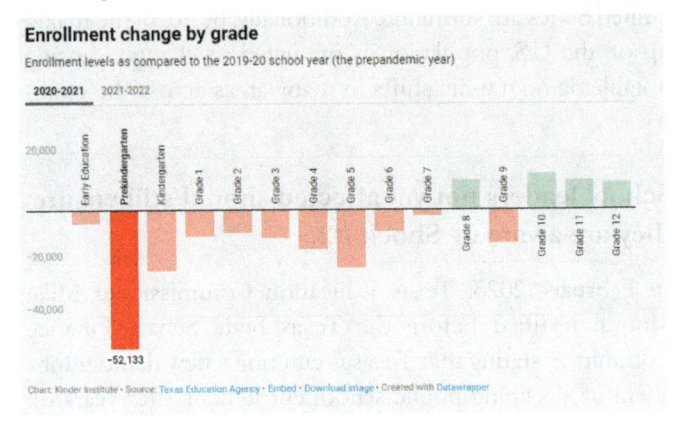

Enrollment change by grade

Enrollment levels as compared to the 2019-20 school year (the prepandemic year)

Source: The Texas Education Agency

This chart by Kinder Institute (Dulin, 2022) reflects the Texas Education Agency's enrollment data showing that pre- pandemic pre-kindergarten enrollment levels decreased by over 50,000 students.

When looking at enrollment data for any particular district or region, it is critical to look at early grade levels now to gain a clear picture of local trends that will shape the next decade.

The pandemic dealt an immediate negative blow to student enrollment, which has not yet recovered. The data set illustrated in the chart below, *Enrollment Changes by How Schools Taught During the Pandemic*, quantifies enrollment decline by "learning mode" in a public school. Of course, the learning mode was the *emergency remote learning* effort to continue school while keeping staff and students safe. It is no wonder emergency remote learning did not work. Staff did their best to engage students and families, but the emergency afforded no opportunity for any preparation for success. In the meantime, the entire community was embattled in efforts to contain the disease, keep it from spreading, and keep people out of the hospital, off of ventilators, and alive. When has a systemic initiative ever been successful under such conditions?

Due to school closures, parents had to rearrange how their children attended school while managing shifting employment circumstances and caring for the elderly as well as children not old enough to attend school. These changes impacted budgets and lifestyles tremendously. Working parents scrambled to find a solution that would allow them to continue to work. At the same time, many parents and caretakers who were already at home scrambled to find a solution for the challenges they were encountering in the emergency remote learning program provided by the public school. This opened the door to more parents deciding to leave the public school system than ever before in history. The data outlines the trend to access non-traditional school models outside the local public school district in 2020.

Enrollment Changes by How Schools Taught During the Pandemic

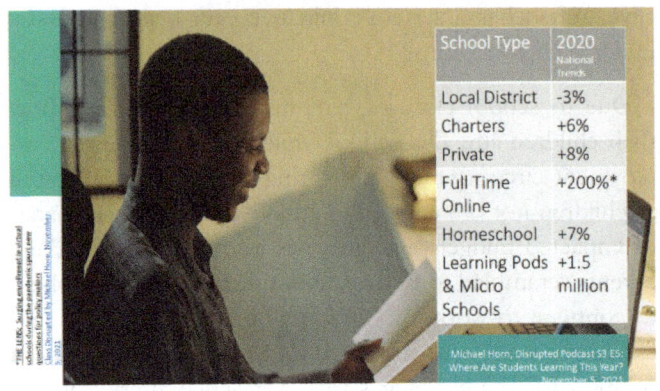

School Type	2020 National Trends
Local District	-3%
Charters	+6%
Private	+8%
Full Time Online	+200%*
Homeschool	+7%
Learning Pods & Micro Schools	+1.5 million

Source: CRPE, and Michael Horn's November 5, 2021 podcast from Class Disrupted

An analysis of the numbers indicates that 40% of the students the local district lost in the shift went to full-time online schools, which grew by 200%. The remaining 60% of students who left the local district went to other school settings, which could have been based on a full-time online school structure but was primarily recognized as a charter, private school, or homeschool. These changes reflect a mammoth swing to full-time online schools and illustrates that this option makes sense to families.

Figure 1. Virtual school enrollment had been rising long before the pandemic

Source: Center on Reinventing Public Education

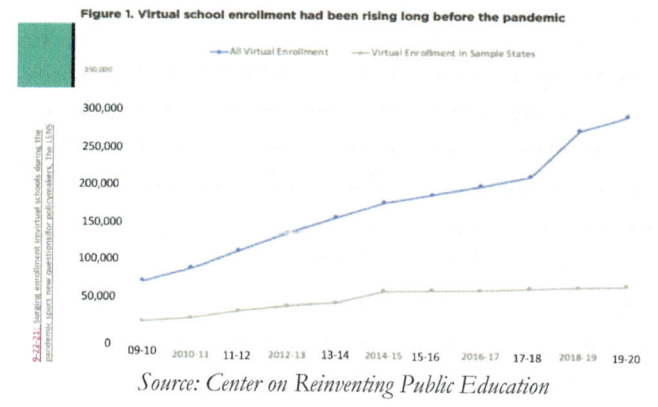

According to the Center on Reinventing Public Education (Gross, 2023), "Surging enrollment in virtual schools during the pandemic spurs new questions for policy makers,"

Virtual school enrollment has been rising for years leading up to the pandemic. (Note: Virtual schools were given a different classification scheme before the 2016–17 school year. For consistency, a backward-looking aggregate enrollment trend for all schools classified in the Common Core of Data as "full virtual" in 2019–20 is shown. Sample states include AR, FL, GA, ME, NH, PA, RI, and UT.)

The blue line in the chart above represents all virtual schools, while the gray line represents virtual-only schools. This indicates that local school districts are starting to figure out how to provide online and virtual schools as part of their systems. States included in the gray line are smaller states like Maine, Utah, Rhode Island, and New Hampshire. The large states in the sample included Florida, Pennsylvania, and Arkansas.

Learning Loss

An unfortunate outcome of the upheaval with school closures and emergency remote learning is the loss of learning that occurred when school attendance was disrupted. As schools began to reopen in 2022, the shared vision was to open the school doors, bring the students in, and "get back to normal." While schools open for face-to-face teaching and learning in a physical building slowly returned to normal, the disruption changed the needs of students and their families. State and federal agencies responded with summative assessment leniency and federal resources.

Many students still have not returned to public schools. There is still so much to uncover related to learning loss and social-emotional well-being in students who have not returned and students who have not yet entered grade levels included in assessments. Stanford Economist Thomas Dee has been tracking this issue. In Harvard EdCast (Anderson, 2023), he states that "some of the most substantial reductions in enrollment are among younger students, [who] won't [test] until we hit the fiscal cliff, when the federal resources available to school districts run out" (para. 2).

Online Learning That Makes Sense to Families

The experience of school leaders of online learning programs that were already operating prior to the pandemic was very different from that of traditional school leaders. Phone calls sky-rocketed from interested parents expressing their fatigue and uncertainty related to options available at their local school. Some were aware of the local options but felt the district was not equipped to teach online. Enrollment in existing online schools quickly spiked as families sought a school already seasoned in online teaching and learning. Enrolling families were concerned that their children were not learning through local emergency remote learning and put their confidence in teachers and administrators who were already experienced and well-trained in the online instructional setting.

During school closures, student withdrawals from full-time online schools stopped while student engagement increased. Looking at existing full-time virtual schools, increased academic gaps and learning loss were not apparent for continuously enrolled online students. Conversely, many staff reported that learning seemed to accelerate as students had fewer distractions outside of school. After school activities had been canceled, students had more time to do their schoolwork.

Students and families longed for the familiar, and for students and families already enrolled in full-time virtual schools, going to school online was familiar. Quality online learning is already designed to include personalized instruction and ongoing interaction between teachers and students and among students. However, staff struggled to keep up with the demands for increased engagement. Educators often shared that they were exhausted juggling new demands at home with their own children and family while, simultaneously, the online students they taught were even more engaged in their classes and, therefore, looking for increased interaction from the teachers and educators supporting them. In many cases, creativity sky-rocketed as teacher teams ramped up support of each other and their students while managing increased personal family needs.

In the meantime, just as parents feared, learning gaps were apparent when those parents whose students were new to virtual learning turned to existing online schools to quickly onboard their children. Often, these parents shared that they were seeking a consistent routine with engaged, experienced online teachers who knew how to address the learning gaps in a virtual learning environment.

As existing full-time online schools with the capacity to grow increased their staff, they found a more robust teacher pool. Many high-quality teachers sought online teaching to be at home with their own children, who were also online, and to increase their personal safety and that of their family through the nature of a virtual versus face-to-face environment.

Through the stories districts have shared, a key takeaway is that many local districts created a one-size-fits-all virtual program that required students to be on a real-time video conferencing platform, such as Zoom, with teachers simultaneously teaching both students who were present in-person in their physical classroom and students participating virtually. Brick-and-mortar counterparts were focused on how to enforce classroom management on the video conferencing platform, including dress code. It became obvious that the more a school focused on online behavior, the less online learning was happening. Of course, this was a profound example of traditional schools doing their best to continue whole-group teaching by pulling students together in Zoom and other similar video conferencing platforms.

At this point, it's very important to clarify the differences between leading a high-quality and accountable online school versus emergency remote learning. The Digital Learning Collaborative (DLC) effectively captures the essential differences in their comparison of emergency remote learning versus online learning, as shown in the chart below.

Contrasting emergency remote learning and online learning

When physical schools closed and instruction shifted from brick-and-mortar classrooms to teaching primarily via live video, many observers said that these schools were now online.

But emergency remote learning looked very different from the instruction that experienced online educators had developed over decades.

EMERGENCY REMOTE LEARNING	VS	ONLINE LEARNING
Implemented with little planning by necessity		Planned for months if not years
Temporary		Short- or long-term, based on the student
For all classes		For any number of classes, from one to all
For most if not all students in a district		For a small subset of students
For most if not all teachers in a district		For a small subset of teachers
Little teacher PD in most cases because of time		Extensive teacher PD and support
Mostly synchronous, group classes		Mostly asynch and/or one on one
Limited onboarding processes for students		Extensive and often standardized onboarding for new students
Coursework delivered to full class		Teachers often personalize learning for each student
Inconsistent communication with families		Communication with families/learning coaches often part of instruction

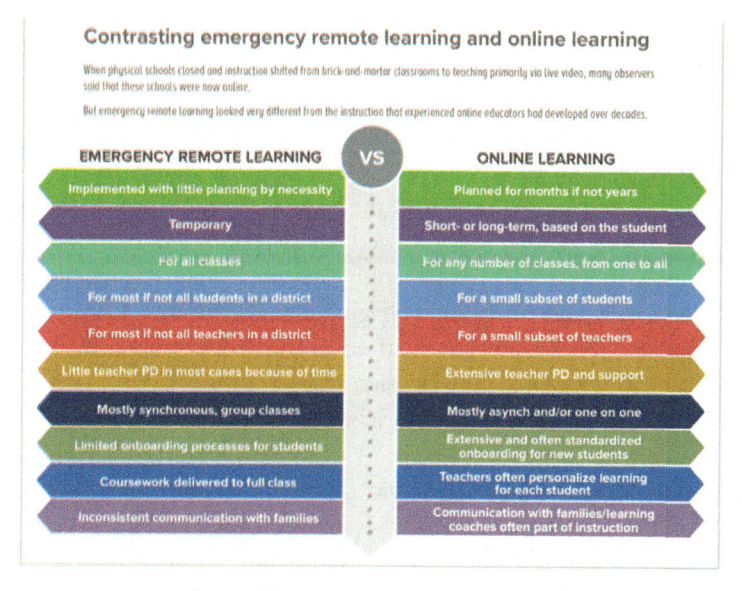

Source: The Digital Learning Collaborative

The Digital Learning Collaborative illustrates the differences between emergency remote learning and high-quality online learning.

Unfortunately, the grave deficiencies of most emergency remote learning tainted many districts' willingness to pursue quality online learning programs. There has been widespread confusion about the differences between the two.

Online learning supports teachers and students in ways not afforded by a traditional brick-and-mortar classroom. The lack of trust instilled through the catastrophic challenges of emergency remote learning deprives many districts of the opportunity to partner with parents who want this option for their children. The flexibility and personalization offered by online learning should be available for those who want this type of schooling. Both public and private school options exist for students and their families if a district does not choose to offer this option locally.

However, caution is warranted when establishing new online schools post-pandemic after emergency remote learning. A general lack of understanding of high-quality and accountable online education exacerbates the challenges of achieving school success. Many post-pandemic online school startups have lacked the necessary foundations for technology and the specialized knowledge related to hiring qualified staff, implementing effective online teaching strategies, and providing engaging digital curricula. Consequently, this has negatively affected the proper onboarding of staff, students, and families, leading to the faltering of many post-pandemic online schools.

Adopting New Pathways

Public school districts now find themselves in a more competitive environment than ever before, so it is critical to offer more learning options—or pathways—including online learning opportunities for students. In a survey done by EdChoice, results indicated that many pathways preferred by parents were not offered by the district their students attended. Additionally, enrollment in charter school networks is expected to increase as charter school networks expand their local campuses. To offer what parents and students are seeking, public schools must provide a variety of learning pathways for students—whether they are planning to go to college or into a career. If the local public school district doesn't offer the desired pathway, parents may look to other education venues.

Offering multiple learning pathways can help the district combat current and future declines in enrollment. If given more options, the parental preferences shown in the graphic below could become the makeup of education. As more options become available, public districts must provide options to entice families to stay.

Parents' Schooling Preferences vs. Actual Enrollment

Where parents *want* to send their kids to school and where they *actually* send their kids to school don't match up.

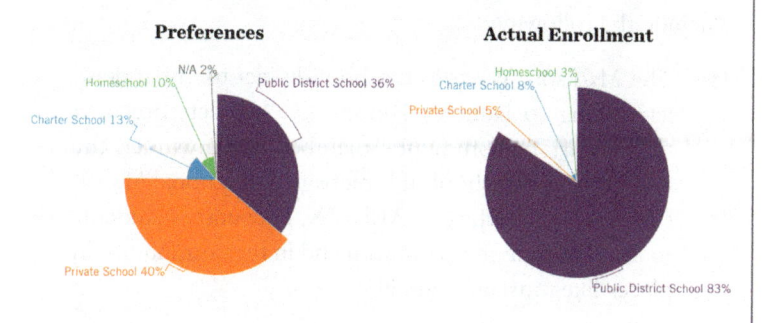

Preferences
- Public District School 36%
- Private School 40%
- Charter School 13%
- Homeschool 10%
- N/A 2%

Actual Enrollment
- Public District School 83%
- Charter School 8%
- Private School 5%
- Homeschool 3%

Source: Edchoice

Edchoice shows how parents would enroll their children if they had a choice. The difference between those who want to send their children to public schools and those who would choose otherwise should be a topic discussed among the local instructional leadership team.

The 74 (Rhodes & Szabo, 2023) reported that parents largely choose their educational experience for their child based on their own experience, without gathering other information. Those with a positive public school experience will likely send their children to public school with no qualms. But parents who had a negative experience are looking for other options. Districts must communicate with families, express the value of their schools, and be clear on what families can expect as their children are enrolled in the district. Parent perspective plays the largest role in this decision, and district leaders cannot assume that parents had a positive experience with their own education.

Longing for Innovation

It is not only parents who want options for students. Teachers want to innovate, too! They often feel they can't because of existing barriers in the educational system. There are several efforts underway across the country to spur innovation. Some examples of innovation cited by The74 (Waite, 2023) include the following:

- The Madison, Wisconsin school district used pandemic funding to launch 14 innovative projects dreamed up by staff or community members. One winner, the antiracist microschool ([Homepage of National Microschooling Center], n.d.) ALL+IN, encourages students to learn outside the classroom and in the community, in places like museums and libraries.

- In North Carolina, the rural Edgecombe County district has used microschools and learning hubs for years to develop and test different school designs.

- In Indiana, Innovation Network Schools support the growth of autonomous schools that operate inside Indianapolis public schools but with flexibilities similar to those enjoyed by independent charter schools.

- Across the country, teacher-powered schools are governed by teams of educators instead of a single principal.

- Microschools like the Black Mothers Forum, Vita Schools of Innovation, Great Hearts Microschools, Arizona State University's ASU Prep microschools, and Gem Prep Learning Societies have launched under the umbrella of a sponsoring charter school.

- Nokomis Regional High School in Maine has created a strong culture of teacher-led innovation with support from administrators.

There are many other strategies also being explored by schools.

- Washington Elementary School, Lindsay Unified School District ([Homepage of Lindsay Unified School District], n.d; [Homepage of Washington Elementary School], n.d.) in California's Central Valley, is a leading example of a personalized and competency-based K–8 (Schools worth visiting, 2023) school. Every student has a personal learning plan and sets daily goals—a great example of developing and engaging student agency and social-emotional learning.

- Highland Academy ([Homepage of Highland Academy], n.d.) in Anchorage is a 6–12 learning environment that promotes mastery learning through integrated project-based learning. Guiding ideas include shared leadership, shared vision, and personal mastery through standards-based instruction with systemic and systematic continuous improvement (featured on Aurora Institute's CompetencyWorks; Sturgis, 2020).

- Across the county, there are more teachers continuing to teach remotely (Will, 2021). In their feedback, they say they feel like actual teachers again, with fewer distractions. Teachers can invite guest speakers and be creative in ways that traditional brick-and-mortar schools can't easily allow.

- Reconfiguring staffing is another innovation helping educators and giving parents more options. Two or more teachers co-teaching a class is one example that gives educators more time to collaborate and, simultaneously, gives students double the knowledge in the room.

- Texas provides an example of a state that has created a Build Your Own Tutoring System_(Texas Education Agency, 2021). Tutoring is a long-proven method for supporting students who need additional time and attention. This additional support and its benefits can be very appealing to families.

- Ideas growing in popularity in large districts are microschools, learning pods, and a "school- within-a-school." These options appeal to families and students because they allow for smaller cohorts, more personalization, and support for socio-emotional needs.
- Smaller districts seek to be more innovative with the school schedule, such as going to a four-day school week.
- Regardless of the size of the school, digital and e-learning options can expand the opportunities available to students while providing more personalized instruction.

Now is a great opportunity for districts to take inventory of their offering and compare it against what is possible. What approaches, services, or learning options are currently available? What aren't? What do local parents and students want? There are many options to consider, including:

- District-run charter schools
- Magnet school(s) for specialized interests
- School-within-a-school models
- Learning pods and microschools_([Homepage of National Microschooling Center], n.d.)
- Innovative instructional practices for students in traditional classrooms and nontraditional settings that include strong digital learning components
- Opportunities for students to take one or more virtual courses onsite or offsite
- Hybrid schools that offer a blended schedule between virtual and brick-and-mortar settings, allowing a stu-

dent to learn onsite some days and at home or offsite other days
- Full-time virtual school options

Open Enrollment Policies

Open-enrollment policies that allow students to attend a public school outside their own residential zone may seem counterintuitive, but open-enrollment policies can actually increase enrollment. This is shown in examples of districts that adopted these open transfer policies and saw increased enrollment even as the local student population declined. In some cases, the additional funds accompanying transfer students helped these districts, often small or rural, stay afloat.

The 74 (Schwalbach, 2023) reports that districts with open enrollment policies have seen increased enrollments were initially hesitant to embrace the concept. Once the policy was fully implemented, districts recognized that it could help attract more students (and the accompanying state funding), support innovation, and provide students with options they would not have had otherwise.

Starting new programs is laborious and taxing on already exhausted staff, but offering the options parents and students want is imperative for long-term sustainability. Post-COVID-19, school leaders, parents, and students want non-traditional choices and support more than ever. This can make setting up a new program easier, as innovation is expected, but also more difficult as quality and accountability must be ensured.

Key Takeaways

Enrollment declines brought about by the pandemic, shifting demographics, school choice, and other forces cannot be undone. The next step is for districts to respond by identifying and implementing positive changes. This will not happen overnight. School districts can earn back the trust that was lost through the dynamics of the pandemic and culture wars. School districts can fortify offerings by adding learning pathways and school choices to attract, engage, and inspire students and the community. School districts can build trust that children will catch up and thrive academically and emotionally in school. Head over to the workbook to think through these variables and nuances with your team to ensure your school is solidly in a category that attracts and keeps students.

CHAPTER 3

SHOCK #3: ONGOING INFLATION AND CHANGES IN THE LABOR MARKET

Attracting & Retaining the Next Generation of Educators

In addition to ongoing inflation, which is discussed further in Chapter 4, one of the painful and persistent fallouts from the COVID-19 pandemic is widespread labor shortages at all levels across nearly all sectors of the economy. Other changes in the labor market impact schools as well. The public sector has long had to be creative in attracting and retaining talent. State health and retirement benefits are still the best in the country. Still, the benefits that once attracted workers to state-related jobs, including jobs in public education, can no longer keep up with the innovative benefits that the private sector continues to introduce.

Additionally, there are several other factors negatively impacting schools' ability in the last few years to attract and retain their most precious asset, human capital. The increased public discourse that isn't so civil, an onslaught of new tools educators are expected to learn to use, and substantial gains in workplace flexibility in other industries that aren't offered in a traditional school environment are the top reasons educators are either leaving or not becoming educators in the first place.

These factors demand a rethinking of options, benefits, and support for teachers, administrators, and staff to attract the next generation of educators into the field and keep experienced ones.

The Future of Education Talent in Numbers

To say education is experiencing workforce challenges is an understatement. The talent pipeline is shrinking. According to a survey (Walker, 2022) conducted by the National Education Association (NEA), "A staggering 55% of educators are thinking about leaving the profession earlier than they had planned. This represents a significant increase from 37% in August 2021 and is true for educators regardless of age or years teaching, driving buses, or serving meals to students" (para. 1). The NEA also pointed out that "According to the U.S. Bureau of Labor Statistics (BLS), there were approximately 10.6 million educators working in public education in January 2020; today, there are just 10.0 million, a net loss of around 600,000" (Survival mode section, para. 1).

On top of those leaving the field of education, there are fewer entering it as well. According to the American Association of Colleges for Teacher Education ([AACTE], 2022), COVID–19 continues to "have a significant effect on undergraduate enrollment, budgets, and staffing" (para. 3). In both fall 2020 and fall 2021, AACTE data shows that 20% of institutions reported that "the pandemic resulted in a decline in new undergraduate enrollment of 11% or more. At the graduate level, 13% of fall 2021 respondents reported significant declines in the number of new graduate students due to the pandemic" (para. 3). Between educators leaving the field and a decrease in those entering, the teacher shortage, which predates the pandemic, is exacerbated even further.

The high number of early exits combined with the alarming decrease in those entering the field makes attracting and retaining talent critical for every district. New strategies are needed to attract new educators and keep current ones. So, how to do that?

Increase Interest by Starting New Learning Models

History tells us the traditional school schedule was established to meet agricultural needs. The traditional 9–5 Monday–Friday work schedule was based on the need to support the standardization of the factory model. We are now in an information era where the power of knowledge and the dissemination of information have become the driving forces shaping our society. Agriculture-based and factory-model standardization-based schedules cannot provide the fluidity needed by students, workers, and families. In addition, there is a reluctance to change school calendars associated with the tourism business and the vacation schedules of young families. School schedules restrict the teaching profession from accessing a more flexible work environment.

Many professions have evolved to offer at least a hybrid approach to work, with one or more days of work at the office and the balance spent working remotely. Many positions are moving to completely remote schedules. In the face of this new marketplace reality, a job that requires an employee to be in the office for 40 hours every week becomes less desirable. How can the education sector break these barriers and compete in the labor market?

Online learning models are one way to create greater flexibility for teachers' work schedules, making it easier for them to schedule time for professional development and alleviate an out-of-kilter work-life balance that contributes to burnout. Time for more personalized instruction is another very important benefit. Online teachers frequently applaud the flexibility virtual learning gives them to get to know their students as individuals.

For years there has been much talk about how educators need to not be the "sage on the stage" but the "guide on the side." So, what if education took that to heart and freed teachers to facilitate more relevant and personalized learning? As districts look to more widespread adoption of such progressive instructional models (personalized, competency-based learning, hybrid and virtual learning), opportunities for educators both to grow professionally and to have more flex time are possible. Are such programs available locally? What are the barriers to beginning these programs or expanding existing ones?

Cross-curricular instruction (Santos, 2022) and project-based learning offer a way for teachers to plan lessons that incorporate more than one disciplinary area. This allows students to broaden their lens of understanding and apply skills and strategies to deepen their overall understanding and make authentic, real-world connections. This approach enables teachers in different disciplines to work together and, in many instances, increases flexibility in the schedule because planning is done together and lessons encompass concepts and skills in multiple disciplines rather than each lesson being planned and created by a single individual, covering only a single discipline. This looks very different from a typical school day and setting, but educators immersed in this model consistently speak to the benefits born from its flexibility.

Other new learning models are emerging that support more flexibility within the teacher's day. For example, districts with community partners can provide students with more relevant educational opportunities that are personalized and highly focused on career goals. One long-standing and successful program is Partners in Education for Business Success, sponsored by Blue Cross Blue Shield (BCBS). The program operates as an informal internship program designed not only to benefit high school students but also to serve as a strategic recruitment tool. In collaboration with Duval and Baker County Schools in Florida, the program targets high school students, offering them hands-on training within their school schedules. BCBS has designated an office and provided a company-appointed supervisor, aligning this initiative with the company's broader employment goals. Students are compensated hourly, allowing them to gain valuable work experience without compromising their high school education. This informal internship is a proactive recruitment strategy. It is particularly advantageous for students in Baker County, a rural district where accessing similar opportunities in nearby Jacksonville is often challenging due to transportation and time constraints. Unfortunately, the current lack of alignment with the state's curriculum hinders students from earning credits in the program. However, addressing this issue is a feasible task, given a strong commitment to collaboration and curriculum alignment.

Other innovative models include blended learning, hybrid schools, and online courses. There are many pathways to flexibility in a teacher's day while strengthening academic and career outcomes for students.

Emerging Technologies

Technology can be a double-edged sword. It will attract some while making others apprehensive. The key is clearly showing the educational benefit and helping apprehensive adopters become comfortable with the technology. While fully online and hybrid options typically take place at least 50% away from a traditional school, there is still plenty of room to consider technology in a more traditional setting. A few very promising areas for success using technology-assisted learning include artificial intelligence (AI), augmented reality (AR), and virtual reality (VR). They each offer innovative ways to help students learn, but they each work differently in the classroom.

Oxford Dictionary **definitions:**

- Artificial intelligence: the theory and development of computer systems able to perform tasks that normally require human intelligence, such as visual perception, speech recognition, decision-making, and translation between languages.

- Augmented reality: a technology that superimposes (Oxford English Dictionary [OED], 2023c) a computer-generated image on a user's view of the real world, thus providing a composite view.

- Virtual reality: the computer-generated simulation of a three-dimensional (OED, 2023d) image or environment that can be interacted (OED, 2023b) with in a seemingly real or physical way by a person using special electronic equipment, such as a helmet with a screen inside or gloves fitted with sensors.

Consider how each of these technology-assisted tools be used to help enhance learning and create new learning models for students and teachers.

Artificial Intelligence

The era of AI in education is just getting started and some encouraging developments are coming to education even as this guide is being sent to the publisher. AI has sparked a great deal of controversy, with some seeing it as a threat to learning and others embracing it as a promising tool for further learning.

A series of blogs written by John Watson and Justin Bruno ("Blog Posts from DLC," n.d.) and published by the DLC tackle the case for and against this intriguing tool. The blog *Will AI transform education? The case for*, written by John Watson (2023), founder, and CEO of Evergreen Education

Group, includes a quote from *The New York Times*, saying the *Times* "published an expansive essay, What Would Plato Say About ChatGPT?", that includes this provocative opening:

'Plato mourned the invention of the alphabet, worried that the use of text would threaten traditional memory-based arts of rhetoric. In his "Dialogues," arguing through the voice of Thamus, the Egyptian king of the gods, Plato claimed the use of this more modern technology would create "forgetfulness in the learners' souls because they will not use their memories," that it would impart "not truth but only the semblance of truth" and that those who adopt it would "appear to be omniscient and will generally know nothing," with "the show of wisdom without the reality.

If Plato were alive today, would he say similar things about ChatGPT?' (Tufekci, 2022, para. 1).

Regardless of where any one person may stand on the issue, AI is now firmly on the scene to stay. Students know it exists, and can be counted on to continue to use it. Teachers are also finding that it can be a valuable resource to help them. So, the most important question about AI in education now becomes, not *if*, but *how* can the use of AI be harnessed to serve teaching and learning?

In a recent Ted Talk by education leader and entrepreneur Sal Khan (2023), *How AI could save Education, not Destroy it* [video], Khan argues that AI can be both a personalized tutor for students and a personal assistant for teachers. The assistance of AI has the potential to provide support for educators and eliminate some of the challenges that lead many to leave the teaching profession. He discusses how AI can move below-average students to average and average students to above-average. (Referencing Benjamin Bloom's "2 sigma problem" which refers to a phenomenon observed in education, specifically in the context of standardized testing. It was first introduced by educational psychologist Benjamin Bloom in 1984. The problem arises when students who receive highly effective instruction perform at significantly different levels than students who receive other types of instruction, leading to a large achievement gap.)

To provide more context, the term "2 sigma" refers to the standard deviation, a statistical measure of variability. Bloom's research found that students who received one-on-one tutoring performed, on average, two standard deviations better than students who received conventional classroom instruction. This significant difference in performance highlights the challenge of achieving similar levels of success for all students within a traditional classroom setting.

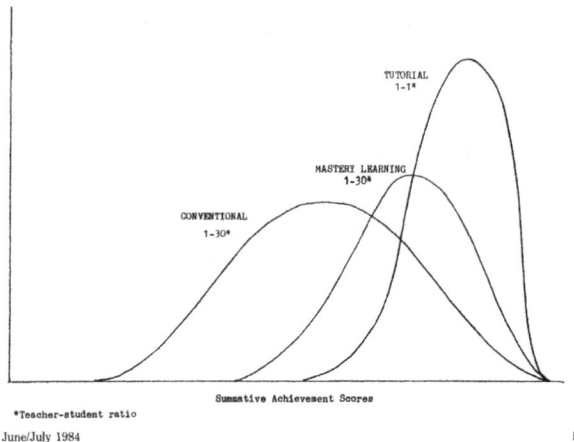

FIGURE 1. *Achievement distribution for students under conventional, mastery learning, and tutorial instruction.*

[Figure showing three overlapping distribution curves labeled CONVENTIONAL 1-30*, MASTERY LEARNING 1-30*, and TUTORIAL 1-1*, plotted against Summative Achievement Scores. *Teacher-student ratio]

Source: Benjamin Bloom, educational researcher

Augmented Reality

According to Maryville University, "Augmented reality (AR) superimposes sounds, videos, and graphics onto an existing environment. It uses four main components to superimpose images on current environments: cameras and sensors, processing, projection, and reflection" (Augmented reality in education, 2023, para. 4).

The clearest and most understood examples of AR to consider are found on Instagram reels and football games. AR shows a background with a GIF or a video of the person themselves superimposed over it. Another common example is the lines and circles drawn on a football field during a televised game. Those lines are not visible in person at the stadium, but if the fan watches the game on television, those AR functions are visible and can be very helpful. This is the same for students. Enhancing curriculum with these same functions can accelerate learning and make it come to life.

There is a difference between augmented and virtual reality. AR can bring to life concepts that may be hard for students to visualize. Some students do not see that math is all around us, through architecture, baking, and even calculating distance as they run around a track. AR helps students see abstract concepts through real-life scenarios. Bringing subjects to life through AR shows great promise for student knowledge in areas that have experienced the largest learning gaps and have been exacerbated even more by COVID-19 school closures.

There are only a handful of studies on the success of using AR, in math specifically, but the results are promising. The National Library of Medicine published a study (AlNajdi, 2022) showing statistically significant improvements in vector geometry after using AR technology.

Virtual Reality

Currently, virtual reality (VR) is used less in the classroom, as there are still some kinks to work out, but a quick online search shows that many districts are willing to dive in and try it. There are pilot schools and pockets of innovation in the main landscape right now. Just as everything in technology improves, virtual reality will keep moving forward as well. Through VR, students can experience being on top of a mountain landscape or in the depths of ocean underwater ecosystems. It allows students to explore and engage with educational content in a more hands-on and experiential way. For example, students who can experience the signing of the Declaration of Independence on July 4, 1776, through VR are much more likely to recall information when being assessed on it.

A study conducted by the University of Maryland (Ventsias, 2021) found that students who learned through virtual reality had significantly higher assessment scores compared to those who learned through traditional methods. Additionally, virtual reality can provide personalized learning experiences tailored to each student's needs, improving assessment scores. However, it is essential to note that the effectiveness of virtual reality in increasing student assessment scores may vary depending on various factors such as the quality of the VR content, the instructional design, and the individual student's learning style and preferences. The impact, as always, is dependent upon the fidelity of implementation.

Think Outside the Box for Benefits

As the private sector continues to offer flexibility for employees, districts are trying to keep up. Four-day workweeks are increasing in popularity across the country in both noneducational sector employment and in schools. Revised district policies typically involve lengthening the remaining four school days after one weekday is cut from schools' schedules, according to an article by *Edsurge* (Tamez-Robledo, 2022). They go on to say that about, "660 schools in 24 states were using four-day weeks before the pandemic caused school closures in 2020, according to a Brookings Institutions estimate, a six-fold increase compared to 1999. It's increased since then" (para. 4). Not only is the four-day workweek a great benefit for staff, but there are a number of tangible benefits for students and their families, too.

Another interesting emerging benefit is the idea of offering services that may have come to market since the last time a district really looked at perks. All employees must balance work and life. Little perks such as offering before and after school stress-reduction programs for employees and homework assistance and tutoring services to help ease some of the burdens of employees' family life can all have great appeal.

Other benefits like providing prepared meals that are ready-to-cook at home or personal training for teachers and administrators provided by some of the school's P.E. teachers or other knowledgeable staff may be attractive to school employees and also build comradery and a sense of community among all participants. As social and emotional learning and mental health also take center stage, districts can offer services to help educators who are struggling emotionally or have family members who are struggling.

District leaders can survey teachers and staff about their needs and preferences, then explore ways to afford and provide services that help with these struggles.

Each district must examine methods to present itself as a more attractive destination for new teachers to seek employment. The challenge is figuring out what the district can offer without incurring additional burdensome costs. A recommended initial action is to initiate a task force responsible for discovering and curating low-cost and no-cost resources to be made accessible to staff.

Some examples of low-cost and no-cost resources include Open Educational Resources Commons: K–12 (OER) Teaching and Learning (K–12 teaching and learning, n.d.) and, We Are Teachers ([Homepage for We Are Teachers], n.d.). The mission of OER Commons: K–12 Teaching and Learning is to break down barriers of affordability, be adapted for purposes of accessibility, and be updated in digital formats for contextual relevance more easily than their proprietary counterparts.

Founded in 2007, We Are Teachers is an online platform that enables teachers and businesses to share, connect, and collaborate using Web 2.0 tools and services. The mission of We Are Teachers is to empower teachers through engagement and collaboration with each other and to support businesses working to promote innovation in education. The site includes an innovative "knowledge marketplace" that enables users to share, sell, and receive recommendations from sponsors on a broad range of teaching tools. The list of these free resources is growing exponentially.

In Attracting and Retaining Teachers Through Creative, Free Perks, Zach DiSchiano (2017) highlights a few Texas districts and their creative solutions. These include local business discounts with special coupons to grocery stores, restaurants, and even department stores. One district dedicated a dry-cleaning delivery service by designating space within the school for drop-off and pickup. The dry-cleaning bill still falls to the employee, but there is the convenience of the onsite drop-off and pickup. Another attractive support for employees is providing before and after-school childcare for their young children. DiSchiano mentions several ways in which districts can fund these initiatives.

The Texas Tribune (McNeel, 2022) published a story on Fort Stockton ISD's solution to a teacher shortage in September 2022, stating, "In West Texas, Fort Stockton's solution to a teacher shortage is a motel. The district is paying big money for teachers and sweetening the deal with low-cost housing" (Subtitle section, para. 1). While teacher shortages are nothing new to rural districts, the pandemic made the problem even worse. In addition to building a dozen brick duplexes for teachers and their families to rent at very affordable prices, the small, far West Texas district purchased and refurbished a local motor court-style hotel as part of their plan to recruit teachers. The plan included higher salaries for teaching positions along with low-cost housing. As a result, the district reports it "filled all of its critical positions."

Edweek (Will, 2023) recently hosted a webinar with three districts working to address their teacher shortages. Districts were thinking outside the norm and came up with a variety of options.

- Offer bonuses—and get creative with them
    - This does not mean offering blanket bonuses but reasonable amounts for recruiting and retention. An EdWeek Research Center (Sawchuck, 2022) survey from last summer found that a quarter of teachers said one-time bonuses between $5,001 and $10,000 would keep them in the profession longer—compared to just five percent who said the same about a one-time bonus of less than $2,000. This also means considering how bonuses are paid out. For instance, it may be beneficial to consider

spacing the bonus throughout the year. That way, if a hire doesn't stay, some sign-on bonus remains in-house.

- Referral bonuses are also on the table to help great educators recruit other great educators.

- Register in-house teaching programs with the U.S. Department of Labor to unlock new federal dollars. (In these programs, the residents, who are college students, are paired with an accomplished teacher and work for a full school year as a paraprofessional before taking on a full-time teaching role.)

- Rethink job fairs—do they need to be in person? Try recruiting from outside the district's typical hiring pool and geographic area.

All three districts agreed that any way to elevate the pressures of the profession is desirable when it comes to finding outstanding educators for their district.

Teacher Licensure Changes

Reviews by Education Week and the Education Commission of the States (Will, 2022) found about "a dozen states that have recently amended—or are considering amending—teacher certification rules. Some are changing the criteria for licensure, others are expanding the qualifying score on state licensing tests, and some are dropping licensure tests altogether." Each state relaxing these requirements believes it will open up opportunities to include hundreds or thousands more educators for the fall.

- California and Oklahoma have removed entry exam requirements.

- Missouri allows passage of an exam if the test-taker is within one standard error of measurement or if they were within a few questions of meeting the qualifying score requirements.

- The Alabama State Board of Education voted to reduce Praxis scores by five points (Biertempfel, 2022) as long as potential teachers "have a 2.75 GPA in their teaching field or complete 100 hours of professional learning" (para. 1).

- New Jersey began implementing a five-year pilot program where "teachers applying for certification do not have to meet certain criteria" (Koruth, 2022, para. 5). The law in New Jersey waives either a minimum grade point average (GPA) requirement or a minimum test score requirement and issues prospective teachers Limited Certificates of Eligibility and Limited Certificates of Eligibility with Advanced Standing.

- Texas has had a law on the books since 1995 that allows a district to issue a school district teaching permit to someone who does not hold a teaching certificate (Education Code, 2015). A teacher employed on a school district teaching permit is not certified by the State Board for Educator Certification. The practice and safeguards are described on the TEA website ("School District Teaching," n.d.).

Thinking beyond any single state, it's about to get much easier for some teachers to keep teaching after moving across state lines, according to Education Week. As of spring 2023 (Will, 2023), ten states have signed on to the Interstate Teacher Mobility Compact—the benchmark needed for the agreement to become active. Now, a teacher who has a bachelor's degree completed in a state-approved program for teacher licensure and has a full teaching license can receive an equivalent license from participating states. That means they can teach in another state without having to submit additional materials, take state-specific exams, or complete additional coursework.

The initial ten participating states are Alabama, Colorado, Florida, Kansas, Kentucky, Nevada, Nebraska, Oklahoma, Oregon, and Utah. Six additional states have legislation pending, and other states are likely to join in the coming years. A handful of states already offer full teacher-license reciprocity, but because those states crafted their policies independently, there are some variations in their rules.

Policymakers hope the compact will increase the supply of teachers in their states and help fill classroom vacancies. It won't be a silver bullet, but the model can reduce the red tape that may deter prospective teachers.

Grow Your Own Programs

The Tennessee Department of Education introduced a Grow Your Own (n.d.) program in January 2022. Tennessee is working to set a new path for education professionals by supporting partnerships between education preparation providers and school districts. The idea is to provide no-cost pathways to encourage more potential educators to enter the teaching profession and build a teacher pipeline. The Tennessee Department of Education awarded $4.5m to the Grow Your Own program in 2021 (TDOE awards $4.5 million, 2023).

Iowa is also considering a Grow Your Own program, which is set up similarly to Tennessee. Also launched in January 2022, the Governor announced the Educator and Paraeducator Registered Apprenticeship program ("Gov. Reynolds Launches," 2022). This program provides up to $40,500 over a three-year period for each high school student who completes the Paraeducator Certificate or Associate's degree model. The DOE will provide up to $47,000 over a two-year period for each paraeducator who completes the bachelor's degree model. Funding will support

- tuition and fees up to $7,000/year for up to three years at a community college;
- tuition and fees up to $17,000/ year for up to two years at a public or private four-year college/university; and
- hourly rate of $12 for high school aides while still in school and 50% of wages that districts currently pay for aides and paraeducators for up to 30 hours per week for 36 weeks.

Texas is another state that created a Grow Your Own (2023) program. The Texas Education Agency (TEA), which oversees PreK–12 public education in the state, created the program to support local education agencies to intentionally build "strong, stable, and diverse teacher pipelines from within their own communities. [Grow Your Own] aims to address teacher shortages in hard-to-staff areas, close demographic gaps between students and teachers, and build interest in the teaching profession among high school students" (para. 1).

TEA's Grow Your Own competitive state grant program addresses two potential approaches or pathways: (1) support for education and training program implementation in high schools and (2) transition of candidates such as paraprofessionals, instructional aides, and long-term substitutes to full-time teaching roles. Grant applications and notice of grant awards (NOGAs) are available for review for all grant cycles under Awardees on the TEA website ("Grow Your Own," 2023).

Planning is critical for a Grow Your Own program, especially in the start-up phase. Evidence shows that some programs have not had enough support for students pursuing this pathway, resulting in shattered dreams and harmful distractions for the high school seniors involved. Just like preparation for the medical field, when some students find they cannot manage the sight of blood, the education field will have students who find they cannot manage the demands of a classroom.

Increase the Desire to Stay

While very few school districts can compete with corporate benefits offered in the private sector, school district human resource departments can be proactive in a number of ways, including Using Stay Interviews to Increase Employee Retention (Dooley, 2022). The purpose of the *stay interview* is to assess the employee's satisfaction with their job and what they want to see done that would encourage them to stay. This strategy involves training the interviewer to separate this interview from employee performance conversations. The stay interview has four questions focusing on the employee's work experience and needs. The interview should be conducted in a neutral location and in a casual manner. Based on data collected from the stay interviews, an action plan should be initiated quickly to address identified opportunities. All employees should be included, even those who are low-performing. School leaders can use this template from Monster.com ("Stay Interview Sample," n.d.) to conduct stay interviews.

Creating succession planning for all levels of the school administration is another progressive way to ensure that teachers are aware of growth opportunities and, therefore, may choose to stay with the district longer rather than leave for other opportunities elsewhere. Succession planning takes the stay interview one step further by formalizing support for employees to grow into positions they wish to pursue. Free resources for succession planning can be found on Indeed.com ("Succession Planning," n.d.).

Professional Learning

Educators are looking for more targeted and personalized learning opportunities. There is much talk about meeting students where they are; now it's time to meet educators where they are. They are more than willing to put in the time if they find the available professional learning opportunities add value. To keep educators fulfilled, they must be given opportunities and experiences that allow them to be challenged and to grow professionally and personally.

In a recent survey done by Interactive Educational Systems Design and released by D2L (Schneiderman, 2022), 1,000 U.S. K-12 teachers and district administrators were asked questions about professional learning (PL). The results of this survey are interesting and challenge some existing assumptions about what teachers do or don't want when it comes to their professional learning.

The survey showed, "A growing educator interest emerging from teachers' pandemic experiences in professional learning is ongoing, on-demand, online, and targeted" (p. 4). However, probably due in part to teachers' limited access to frequent and personalized professional learning, the survey reports that "only 20% of surveyed educators identified strong satisfaction with the professional learning opportunities made available by their school and district" (p. 4). That only 20% of educators, who likely identify as lifelong learners, are satisfied with their professional learning opportunities is significant and alarming.

Another significant statistic from the survey shows that district leaders often perceive time as a barrier, while educators do not cite time as a barrier. When professional development gives value to the educator, time is not the issue. The educators also clarified that they would be willing to participate in professional development sessions delivered online, in contrast to district leaders who believe this option would not be utilized.

The same D2L survey found that "71% [of educators] identified interest in professional learning that is online, on-demand (e.g., video segments, learning modules, courses), with 55% indicating their interest increased since the pandemic started" (p. 4).

Districts across the country are working to create professional development playlists, the same concept as teachers creating playlists for their students to differentiate instruction. The playlists include everything from things to watch to things to listen to and read.

District leaders can support their educators by discussing which opportunities they are interested in and how, when, and where they would like professional learning opportunities delivered. It's the best way to discover what educators want and may also lead to ideas about less expensive and more engaging ways to deliver these opportunities.

A report released by the Wallace Foundation (DeWitt Wallace-Reader's Digest Fund, 1997) shows that states can take steps to proactively retain strong teachers after investing in their development. By taking a cue from North Carolina and Texas, the report states that "education chiefs can create advanced certification designations for teachers with outstanding evaluations. These certifications, which come with additional pay, indicate that teachers are ready for advanced responsibilities, such as mentoring apprentices or early-career teachers" (Candal, 2023, para. 6).

This indicates that advanced certification can incentivize high-performing teachers to go where the shortages are more critical, and student performance is typically lower. This new understating can lead states to consider adding a state-funded salary increase to teach in high-need districts.

Making playlists and meeting teachers where they are with professional development as a recruitment and retention tool is smart. However, the organization must have strong leadership to navigate the professional development and support that teachers want versus the ever-growing, mandated lists of annual training that must be completed each year.

Legislatively mandated training will further develop teachers and staff as professionals who are ready to respond to child abuse and neglect effectively, student health and well-being (the use of an Epi-Pen, defibrillator, conducting CPR, bullying, gender identity, blood pathogens, etc.) or crisis management (intruder, campus lockdown, active shooter). But this is not the ongoing development teachers and staff are searching for to stay energized and motivated.

Teacher evaluation, federally funded programs, state testing, grading guidelines, and integration of new technology systems at the school add another layer of necessary training. The sheer volume and complexity of all these elements can be overwhelming and demotivating.

A comprehensive Professional Learning Plan (PLP) is an important component of providing effective leadership that inspires opportunities for teachers to grow and prosper individually. A comprehensive PLP used as a recruitment tool also ensures opportunities for teachers to be clear on employment requirements and grow in their careers based on options that support the district's beliefs, objectives, parameters, and strategies. Identifying the district's beliefs, objectives, parameters, and strategies will set the PLP up to hit a home run for retaining and recruiting staff.

Leadership guidance for PLPs can be found on the LearningForward website (Professional Learning Plans: A Workbook for States, Districts, and Schools; Killion, 2013) and the Hanover Research Website (District Leaders' Guide for Developing a Professional Learning Plan, 2023). An exemplar PLP can be found on the Clear Creek ISD Website (Professional Learning Plan, 2022). Clear Creek's PLP is very intentional in pulling together multiple facets of the ever-growing list of state-mandated training and professional development for innovative programs such as blended and personalized learning.

Create Opportunities for Future Leaders

In addition to a critical teacher shortage, there is also the issue of a shrinking principal pipeline within districts. In many instances, the teachers and staff see their principals under immense stress, discouraging them from wanting to pursue the role. This creates an obvious conundrum. Principals are expected to know how to manage the budget; ensure that deep learning is happening and students do well on state assessments; manage school safety; navigate social discourse; be creative in grappling with a teacher shortage; consider new technology; and compete in the school choice environment. While it's important to meet teachers where they are with a PLP, it's also critical to build a PLP that provides a pipeline for aspiring principals.

How is it possible to incorporate the concept of a principal pipeline into the organization's PLP? Simply put, the principal pipeline is a program to develop effective school leaders that allows staff to express their interest and be selected to participate. In addition to motivating staff to aspire to the principalship, a program like this has astounding benefits.

A groundbreaking report by RAND (Gates et al., 2014) on the success of six large school districts that implemented a program to develop principals. These districts saw significant improvements in student achievement across their communities. After three years, schools in these pipeline districts with newly-appointed principals performed better in reading by over six percentile points and in math by almost three percentile points compared to schools in other districts. This achievement was considered remarkable because there were no other district-wide initiatives that had demonstrated such substantial positive effects on student performance.

Additionally, the principal pipelines contributed to better principal retention. After three years, pipeline districts experienced nearly eight fewer instances of principal turnover for every 100 newly-appointed principals compared to the comparison group. This is significant because high principal turnover disrupts schools and is expensive, costing districts an estimated $75,000 to replace a principal.

While embedding a principal pipeline into the local PLP, be open to emerging technologies that can be incorporated, including thinking through how new and emerging technology, such as simulations (Woodbridge, 2019) can help potential leaders think through likely scenarios that a principal or district leader might encounter.

Those who desire to be superintendents also need support to grow into that role. In an article published by Edweek (Schwartz, 2023), three superintendents recommend the following to build a superintendent pipeline:

- Create opportunities for leaders to build their skills and demonstrate their capabilities
- Pay attention to diversity
- Prepare career educators for a major shift in job duties

These strategies may seem simple and obvious. However, district leaders must be intentional with succession planning through their mentorship and identification of potential leaders, some of whom may not yet even see it in themselves. Failing to plan for succession is a plan to fail, as noted by Siri Akal Khalsa (2017) in Succession Planning: Getting it Right. While most succession planning processes for schools are focused on the school leader hired by the school board, succession planning should dip down into all administrative positions within the district using modified processes offered through teacher leadership programs.

Superintendents and principals have much to share about their first year in leadership, where—no doubt—they suddenly had to deal with issues and situations they never imagined.

As leaders learn to be shock absorbers, the knowledge must be passed on to those who take on this role in the future.

Personnel Cost Considerations

It may also be necessary to review approaches related to personnel costs. There are a variety of options to consider, including:

- Condense the steps within the pay scale. For example, Baker School District (Sierra, 2023) simplified a 14-step pay scale down to just a four-step scale. It meant teachers would start at a higher salary in the district and reach the apex faster. The design also guaranteed every current teacher would get a raise.

- Shift funding distribution between categories of personnel functions, prioritizing functions that support the current educational goals and needs of the district and students the most.

- Take advantage of attrition by implementing a hiring freeze. By not replacing educators and staff who choose to leave the district, the need for layoffs after the federal funds for recurring salaries are no longer available may be prevented or lessened.

- Offer a financial incentive to those who may be willing to consider leaving the district voluntarily and/or coordinate with another district that is having difficulty filling open positions and would be able to offer a hiring bonus to the departing employees.

- Decrease the percentage level or adjust the schedule of raise increases to allow the district to retain more positions.

- Allow job sharing where it's mutually advantageous to specific employees and the district.

Key Takeaways

The traditional approach to offering employee benefits and perks is no longer as effective in attracting and retaining talent as it once was. There are many options to consider in trying to combat this. This shift is especially important because millennials now constitute one-third of the workforce. When hiring and retaining personnel, school districts need to adapt to this changing landscape and workforce.

In this competitive environment, industries that can find ways to alleviate some of life's challenges for their employees will gain a significant edge in attracting and retaining top talent. It's now the responsibility of school districts to think imaginatively and devise solutions that resonate with this new generation of workers. Head over to the workbook to think through creative solutions with your team.

CHAPTER 4
SHOCK #4: AN ECONOMIC SLOWDOWN (RECESSION)

Some alarming factors that are currently at play, including inflation, bank failures, and labor scarcity, feed into financial experts' expectations that the country is headed for an economic slowdown or recession.

Inflation

Inflation is a phenomenon that occurs when the general price level of goods and services in an economy increases over time. It's an essential aspect of any economy and can impact society in numerous ways. Not only does inflation impact employees in the district, the cost of goods and services, and the cost of living, but it also has a big impact on budgets in general.

One of the ways in which inflation impacts school districts is through its effect on the budget allocated to retirement systems and pension plans. (Regardless of the differences between the two, these methods of providing retirement pay are often simply referred to as "pensions.") Pensions are financial arrangements by which a company or government agency provides income for its employees after they retire. In most cases, employees pay into a pension fund throughout their career, and the employer pays its share into the same fund. Inflation diminishes the value of these funds, which can lead to the pension fund being unable to provide the same standard of living it did before. This means more funds must be allocated to pension plans to keep the same level of purchasing power.

A new report from Equable Institute (Randazzo & Moody, 2023) shows that "rising pension costs are slowly eating up a larger and larger share of education budgets. After adjusting for inflation, teacher pension costs have roughly tripled over the last two decades, rising from $21.8 billion in 2001 to $63.7 billion in 2021" (p. 8). However, increased costs have not translated to increased benefits for teachers and other school district employees. In fact, the report shows that, "states have been systematically reducing the value of their benefits in response to the rising costs" (Aldeman, 2023, para. 3).

Ed Finance experts at Allovue (Gartner et al., 2022) note that, in the decade between fiscal years 2009 and 2019 (adjusting all figures for inflation)

- "K–12 education spending increased 9%;
- total pension spending increased 90%; and
- pension debt payments increased 240%.

The rising cost of pension debt is taking up an increasing proportion of education budgets, which makes it harder to increase teacher salaries or any other budget line items" (What we can learn from the numbers section).

Pensions can be underfunded for several reasons, including investments that aren't doing well, market and labor shifts, and, as just alluded to, increased interest on the debt itself.

Underfunded pensions must be taken seriously.

Some states pay all or most of retirement costs themselves, while others are paid for by districts. Retirement costs pose a huge liability to districts. When general funding from the state does not increase as costs do, states are not adequately funding education when they may be providing more funds than ever. Suppose a district is taking on more of the cost of retirement. In that case, district leaders should be having conversations with policymakers to ensure they understand that the district is obligated to pay the increased pension cost, which may outstrip an increase in state dollars to the district.

This must not be a political conversation. California holds one of the highest amounts of unfunded liabilities. That being said, Governor Newsom proudly stated that California had a $97.5 billion surplus in the budget without acknowledging the pension debt the state needs to address. It may not be popular to cut a proposed bonus or pay raise, but in the long run, it can open up funds for the district that would have been eaten away by interest rates.

In Louisiana, a budget battle that wasn't settled until the last wild 30 minutes (O'Donoghue, 2023) of the session saw a compromise giving educators a $1,000 raise but also cutting $690 million of public retirement debt. Proponents believe this will free up budgets in the coming years as the interest saved can go directly back to districts.

Inflation has certainly raised interest rates, and anywhere a district can pay down debt will be beneficial as the economy slows.

In 2018, the Teacher Retirement System of Texas, which is among the nation's largest retirement systems, was faced with a pension fund liability that would have required 87 years to amortize. In 2019, the state legislature enacted a plan via Senate Bill (SB) 12 that began scheduled contribution rate increases to help the pension fund move closer to full funding. According to a report by the pension's actuarial firm, "SB 12 policies ... will save the state significant money over the long term" (Fresh Picks, 2022, para. 8).

Texas has also taken steps to improve the state's Employee Retirement System (ERS) for all state employees, including employees of TEA, the state's PreK–12 public education agency. In 2023, following up on steps taken in the previous legislative session, the Texas legislature appropriated $900,000,000 from the state's general revenue fund to continue efforts to address ERS' unfunded actuarial liabilities.

States across the country must apply meaningful financial support to pension systems supporting educators and state education department employees to avoid potentially catastrophic costs to the state resulting from unfunded pension system liabilities. The next graph gives a great picture of how pension debt costs are continually rising and cutting into more of the operating budget each year.

TEACHER RETIREMENT COST HISTORY

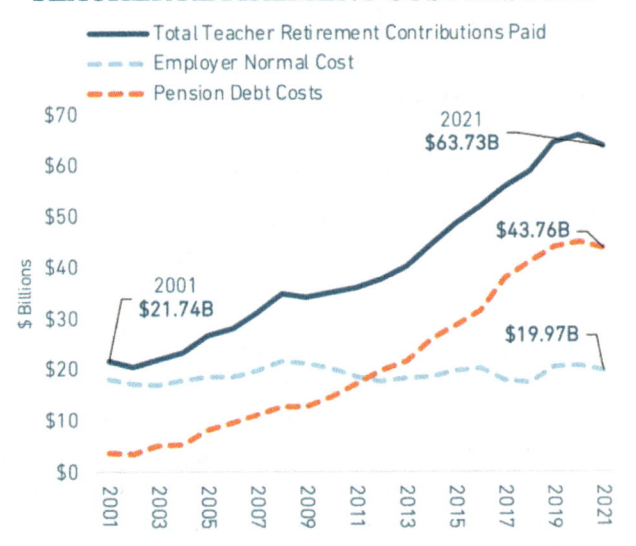

- Total Teacher Retirement Contributions Paid
- Employer Normal Cost
- Pension Debt Costs

2001: $21.74B
2021: $63.73B
$43.76B
$19.97B

Source: Equable Institute analysis of public plan valuation reports and ACFRs. Data are adjusted for inflation to 2021 dollars.

As published by The 74 (Aldeman, 2023) the Equable Institute shows that rising pension costs are slowly eating up a larger and larger share of education budgets. After adjusting for inflation, teacher pension costs have roughly tripled over the last two decades, rising from $21.8 billion in 2001 to $63.7 billion in 2021.

Pension costs still represent just a fraction of overall education spending. However, because these costs are rising so much faster than everything else, true education spending is not growing as fast as it appears. Equable (Randazzo & Moody, 2023) dubs these "America's Hidden Education Funding Cuts."

The future of public employee retirement systems will likely involve a combination of innovation and reform. Specifically, some possible areas of innovation could include the use of digital technologies to streamline administrative processes and improve member engagement. Other potential innovations could include exploring more flexible retirement benefit designs. Additionally, public retirement systems may work to enhance their investment strategies by incorporating a wider range of asset classes or leveraging advances in data analytics and algorithmic trading to improve investment returns. Overall, the future of public employee retirement systems will depend on various factors, including demographic trends, economic conditions, and ongoing efforts to improve system sustainability and adaptability.

Another way in which inflation is impacting districts is through its effect on the cost of paying active employees. Like its counterparts in business and industry, salaries are one of the most significant expenses any district will face, and inflation can cause this cost to skyrocket. This means that the district must allocate more funds to maintain the same level of employee compensation and expected raises.

Inflation can also make employee retention more challenging for districts. A salary that is too low can prompt employees to leave for other jobs with better compensation. Due to the rising cost of living, employees will increasingly need to seek higher-paying jobs to better support themselves and their families. Replacing lost employees is expensive. Not only are there many expenses related to hiring and training replacements, but morale and performance in the workplace are negatively impacted.

In addition to the impact on pensions and salaries, as inflation increases, the cost of everything goes up, including the cost of the goods and services the district requires.

Bank Failures

In addition to the threat inflation continues to impose on the likelihood of an economic slowdown, there have been three bank failures thus far in 2023 in the United States. This is adding another impact and burden on districts. "Already under fire for high pay despite big investment losses, the pension system for Ohio's retired teachers lost between $27 million and $40 million when Silicon Valley Bank failed last weekend. That appears to be by far the biggest investment by a public pension system in the United States" (Schladen, 2023, para. 1). The rising cost of pensions and modern-day bank runs, amplified by social media, certainly inspires much prudence and is something district leaders must continue to consider.

Labor Scarcity

Labor scarcity refers to a situation involving a shortage of qualified workers in the labor market. It is typically caused by an imbalance between the demand for workers and their supply. In recent years, labor scarcity has become a significant issue across industries, including many school districts, as employers struggle to find quality talent to fill open positions. Although exacerbated by the COVID-19 pandemic, this phenomenon is driven by several other key factors, including changes in demographics, shifts in education levels, and a mismatch between the skills required of workers and those possessed by job seekers. The labor scarcity can translate into higher wages and benefits, which can contribute to inflation and create an even greater struggle for districts to manage their budgets effectively.

Inflation and labor scarcity are inextricably linked—they affect one another in many ways. When and where the demand for labor is higher than the supply, workers have more bargaining power. They can demand higher salaries for their work because they have more opportunities locally and through relocation. This could strain the district since it will have to allocate more funds to compensate for the higher wages.

Inflation and labor scarcity also affect each other in other ways. Higher inflation leads to an increase in the cost of living, which can discourage workers from residing in localities with lower pay. These workers may then decide to look elsewhere for employment opportunities with better pay. This can reduce the overall labor supply in the district, making it even harder for the district to hire and retain employees.

Inflation continues to impact districts significantly by affecting the budget allocated to pensions, increasing the cost of paying active employees, and making it even harder to retain high-caliber personnel. This, combined with the scarcity of workers in many areas and the increased cost of living, makes it even harder to source and retain good talent. These factors create an unavoidable financial burden on districts to create and maintain competitive compensation plans that sustain their workforces.

There are many considerations for mitigating challenges related to an economic slowdown or recession. Examples of actions that can be taken include the following:

- Understand the solvency of the state retirement system.

- Advocate to help ensure state legislators understand that even if they give schools a larger budget, if they then vote to raise district contribution rates, they may be more than erasing any "extra" budget they voted to give.

- Consider the best strategy to maximize interest rates earned on monies under the district's control to help budgets in the future.

- Use a risk manager when considering how and where to invest dollars under the district's control.

- Set reasonable investment return targets.

- Avoid being overly aggressive in investments–even if it might look better in the short term. Think long term.

Key Takeaways

This shock includes several factors that districts don't have much control over but will still have a big impact on district operations. Inflation, pensions, and bank failures can seem like variables that district leaders just have to accept. However, many of these factors can be addressed with advocacy work and financial planning. Head over to the workbook to discuss areas that could be addressed at the district level, areas that need to be advocated for at the state level, and financial planning steps to ensure district dollars go as far as they can.

CHAPTER 5
TIME TO STRATEGIZE!

The four shocks headed our way give us a lot to contend with. It is true. But the challenges that come along with educating our country's children—tomorrow's leaders—have always been, well, challenging. Consider some strategies in this guide and accompanying workbook to help you devise a path forward.

This is a primer. There is so much more to consider and think through, and it will take more conversations to turn these ideas and strategies into a reality. Each district's path will look different and have many nuances to consider. The shifting education market will require new thinking beyond the buzzwords of innovation and transformation. The pockets of innovation within education have shown us that there are personalized and effective ways to change student lives. This is the time to act based on local needs, start changing deeply rooted systems, and begin working anew for all students with fresh eyes on what can work in the hard realities facing education today.

Consistently Winning Strategies

The consistently winning strategies can easily be boiled down to a few that heavily impact the success of programs and initiatives. These are evident in the changes districts make to their ESSER plans and the examples shared about programs and initiatives with demonstrated results. Consistently winning strategies are rooted in building and fostering relationships and personal connections, keeping students first by personalizing their learning path, and putting innovation into action.

Building Relationships and Personal Connections

Personal connections are key. In almost every aspect of life, it is the personal connections that make the biggest difference. We all know the critical difference one teacher or one caring adult can make in the life of a child. We've all seen it. We've witnessed the power of it.

Looking at some of the adjustments to ESSER funding plans indicates that a trend in consistently winning strategies is to put a high premium on human connections and needs. Recognizing the importance of strong, positive personal connections and using that knowledge to reach students and support families and educators is critical. One way or another in consistently winning strategies, the focus is on building relationships and meeting students and educators where they are to help get them where they need and aspire to be.

The strength of personal connection, or the lack thereof, influences us tremendously. Whether it's deciding where to live, send our children to school, work, or shop, relationships often matter most. Relationships deeply influence our lives, personal growth, motivation, determination, and overall happiness. Think about the relationships between teachers and students, among students, and within school leadership and teachers. Connecting school leaders and teachers to parents and families is crucial. Personal connections are paramount.

What happens between a teacher and a student and among students in the classroom—be it a physical classroom or virtual classroom—is the heart of education, the heart of learning. Great teachers need the support of great school leadership, a strong community with their peers, and professional development that meets their individual needs, delivered at the time and in the manner best for them. All students, families, and educators need a school environment that puts students first and focuses on building and sustaining the personal connections needed for learning to flourish. Families that feel connected to their student's schools are much more likely to stay in the district and invest their critically important parental involvement.

A common focus on supporting personal connections includes increased emphasis on the following things:

- Student-centered, additional instructional time with skilled, caring adults in the form of
  - tutoring programs;
  - intervention programs, especially in math and reading–
    - face-to-face;
    - online;
    - small group; and
    - tiered;
  - extended "Saturday Success" and summer school programs; and
  - mobile classrooms
- Social-emotional support programs for students and educators
- Increased numbers of staff, including teachers, learning and intervention specialists, and instructional aids
- Increased supplemental and other pay for staff

Another winning strategy is for the district or campus to identify where to put needed technology into place to accomplish the following:

- Gather and manage data that will help administrators and teachers understand where and how to target resources

- Support and equip teachers and students to extend learning beyond the school day and campus boundaries and to facilitate communication and connection

The four shocks coming to education are causing things to shift every day. If a district determines that ESSER funds, once allocated to a particular project or approach, need to shift before the September 2024 obligation deadline, this guide and the authors' ongoing work offer ideas and strategies to identify and prioritize new and adjusted approaches, projects, and programs. These resources will also support the use of available funds to mitigate some of the shocks coming, not only when the ESSER deadline passes but also beyond the fiscal cliff.

Keeping Students First and Personalizing Their Learning Paths

The districts that are attracting students are focused on student learning and futures. They're finding flexible models, creating opportunities for career exploration and community relationships, and taking risks in the name of meeting students where they are in their learning. These strategies also attract parents who care deeply about the district.

Putting Innovation into Action

The word innovation is used frequently in education. It has become a buzzword that creates the illusion that it's happening everywhere. The only way for us to have radically different outcomes is to do things in radically different ways. Innovation means trying fresh ideas and, perhaps, taking big risks. This can be done while being smart and finding data for evidence-based interventions. Of course, accountability must still be in place, but accountability must not prohibit doing things differently. Consider the PACE Pilot Program

("Performance Assessment," n.d.) in New Hampshire. In short, there were two systems of assessments taking place at the same time to prove the fidelity of a new system. Innovation can sometimes mean doing more work, but in the end, it will pay off for students and staff.

Ready or not, the shocks are coming to the education market. But you don't have to be shocked. Instead, become the shock absorber who will help your district thrive even in a market where everything around you is on shifting sand!

Not every strategy within this guide will apply to each district, but they can help you stop, think, and get your wheels turning on how you could do things differently. Think creatively. It's the only way to absorb the significant shocks that are coming!

Whichever paths pique your interest, the authors are here for you to continue the conversation. With a bit of help from looking back at history and a clear-eyed assessment of the present, we can create a less "shocked" future and thrive!

We look forward to connecting with you through Become.A.Shock.Absorber@gmail.com and seeing your results with #becomeashockabsorber.

ABOUT THE AUTHORS

Susan Gentz is an experienced policy specialist who began her career working on education policy both as a former staffer in the Iowa House of Representatives and the United States Senate.

Along with experience at both federal and state levels, she served as the Deputy Executive Director for the Center for Digital Education, tracked education issues for a government relations firm in Arlington, VA, and was a policy manager at iNACOL (now the Aurora Institute), where she wrote reports to move the field forward with innovative learning models, best practices, and policy recommendations. She has helped districts, charters, industry partners, and nonprofits with advocacy efforts and has assisted in finding, writing, and winning several grants for partners. As the founder of BSG Strategies and partner at K20Connect she has opportunities to advise clients on opportunities in both state and federal legislation. Her policy thoughts and ideas have been featured in Tech & Learning, Fast Company, the American School Board Journal (NSBA magazine), Converge, and several other media outlets.

Gentz is based in the Des Moines Metro area (Iowa). In her free time she enjoys a solid park day with her three young children, party planning, and explaining the difference between sweet corn and field corn to folks who did not grow up in Iowa...and surprising those same people when she knows nothing about potatoes.

Lea Ann Lockard is an education leadership consultant and president of Elevate e-Learning LLC. Lea Ann delivers strategic consulting services to support school systems in providing high-quality and accountable virtual school and hybrid solutions to meet the dynamic needs of today's students and their families. Elevate-e-Learning.com will support school systems in leveraging resources to meet continuous improvement goals so that remote learners excel.

Lea Ann is the founding principal of Texas Connections Academy (TCAH) and served as the school's leader from June 2009 to June 2021. From 2013 until she retired from the school's leadership in 2021, she was the Executive Director. TCAH is a Texas Virtual School Network Full-Time Online School that offers 100% virtual instruction to public school students across Texas in grades 3–12 who are not physically present on campus during instruction. During her tenure at TCAH, Lea Ann shepherded the school to an annual enrollment of over 8,100 students. During her tenure with Connections Academy, Lea Ann received recognition from EdTech Digest as one of the Top 100 Influencers in 2017, the EdTech Digest Leadership Award Winner in 2016, the United States Distance Learning Association's Outstanding Leadership by an Individual in the Field of Distance Learning in the online technology/K–12 education category in 2014, and Connections Academy's Principal of the year in 2014.

Before joining Connections Academy, Lea Ann was a principal and teacher in Spring Branch ISD where she was the administrator for several district-wide programs including the School Age Parent Program, the academic and disciplinary alternative programs, an over-age eight grade program, and a night school for adult students.

Kate Loughrey, founder of K Loughrey Enterprise, is an education leadership consultant specializing in digital education. She provides expertise to national, state, and district leaders, researchers, and policy makers, helping them fulfill their key roles in digital learning.

As a guest lecturer for the Harvard Graduate School of Education, Kate interacted with international students and up-and-coming digital learning leaders. Her expertise has also been sought at many national and international conferences and symposiums, as well as state, regional, and district-level forums.

Kate served as the statewide coordinator for the Texas Education Agency's (TEA's) online learning initiative, the Texas Virtual School Network. She developed and managed Texas' first online and blended learning pilots before spearheading the state's supplemental and full-time virtual education programs. Among the early pioneers in the field, she brings more than 30 years of leadership experience to the ongoing evolution of digital learning.

Kate led projects to explore innovative learning models, resulting in reports and policy recommendations to the Texas Legislature. She developed great rapport with state and school district leaders, innovators exploring the world of digital learning, and parents seeking the best options for students. She served as the state affiliate member to the Digital Learning Collaborative (DLC) and was on the Southern Regional Education (SREB) committee that created the original national standards of quality for online courses and teaching. These standards became the foundation for subsequent iterations used today.

Prior to her tenure at TEA, Kate worked for the Austin, Texas PBS station as a television producer, writer, and on-air host for programs addressing a wide variety of topics, including public education, arts, civic affairs, and social issues—including an award-winning series on caregiving.

AUTHORS' CONTACT INFORMATION

If you have questions or would like further assistance from the team, please contact us at: become.a.shock.absorber@gmail.com

REFERENCES

[Homepage]. (n.d.). Aurora Institute. https://aurora-institute.org/

[Homepage]. (n.d.). Highland Academy. https://www.asdk12.org/highlandacademy

[Homepage]. (n.d.). Lindsay Unified School District. https://www.lindsay.k12.ca.us/

[Homepage]. (n.d.). National Microschooling Center. https://microschoolingcenter.org/

[Homepage]. (n.d.). U.S. Bureau of Labor Statistics. https://www.bls.gov/

[Homepage]. (n.d.). Washington Elementary School. https://washington.lindsay.k12.ca.us/

[Homepage]. (n.d.). We Are Teachers. https://www.weareteachers.com/

Aldeman, C. (2023, March 21). *Teacher pension Pac-man: How rising costs are eating away at education budgets.* The74. https://www.the74million.org/article/teacher-pension-pac-man-how-rising-costs-are-eating-away-at-education-budgets/

AlNajdi, S. M. (2022). The effectiveness of using augment reality (AR) to enhance sutdent performance: Using quick response (QR) codes in student textbooks in the Saudi education system. *Educational Technological Research and Development, 70*(3), 1105–1124. https://doi.org/10.1007/s11423-022-10100-4

American Association of Colleges for Teacher Education. (2022, February 2). *Survey shows positive trends and lingering effects of COVID in educator preparation.* https://aacte.

org/2022/02/survey-shows-positive-trends-and-lingering-effects-of-covid-in-educator-preparation/

American Rescue Plan Act Elementary and Secondary School Emergency Relief (ARP ESSER): LEA plan for use of ARP ESSER funds, ARP section 2001(e). (2022, June 8). KIPP Delta Public Schools. https://kippdelta.org/wp-content/uploads/2022/08/KDPS-ESSER-ARP-Spending-Plan.pdf

Anderson, J. (2023, April 7). *Where have all the students gone?* Harvard Graduate School. https://www.gse.harvard.edu/ideas/edcast/23/04/where-have-all-students-gone

ARP ESSER III Spending Plan (2022). Norfolk Public Schools. https://www.npsk12.com/Page/17920

Augmented reality in education: Interactive classrooms. (2023, December 6). Maryville University. Retrieved December 28, 2023, from https://online.maryville.edu/blog/augmented-reality-in-education/

Biertempfel, M. (2022, July 12). *AL board of education votes to change teacher certification requirements due to staff shortages*. CBS42. Retrieved December 28, 2023, from https://www.cbs42.com/news/al-board-of-education-votes-to-change-teacher-certification-requirements-due-to-staff-shortages/

Blog posts from DLC members and guests. (n.d.). Digital Learning Collaborative. https://www.digitallearningcollab.com/bloglp

Bloom, B. S. (1984). The 2 sigma problem: The search for methods of group instruction as effective as one-to-one tutoring. *Educational Researcher, 13*(6), 4–16.

Bond, E. W. (2021, July 27). *American Rescue Plan (ARP) Act Elementary and Secondary School Emergency Relief (ESSER) fund III plan*. Augusta County Public Schools. https://core-docs.s3.amazonaws.com/documents/asset/uploaded_

file/1423055/LEA_ARP_ESSER_III_Plan_-_07.27.2021.pdf

Candal, C. (2023, May 15). *Reinvigorating the teacher workforce: Five actions states can take now*. ExcelinEd. Retrieved January 9, 2024, from https://excelined.org/2023/05/09/reinvigorating-the-teacher-workforce-five-actions-states-can-take-now/

Cartwright Elementary School District (070483000) public district—FY 2021—Elementary and secondary school emergency relief (ESSER III) fund—Rev 2—Elementary and secondary school emergency school relief (ESSER III) fund grant. (2023, January 6). https://about.burbio.com/weekly-updates/burbio-school-tracker-3/20-changes-in-virginia?hs_amp=true

Chronic absenteeism: 2017–2023. (2023, December 14). Return2Learn Tracker. Retrieved December 23, 2023, from https://www.returntolearntracker.net/

Deadlines and announcements. (2024, January 9). Department of Education, Office of Elementary & Secondary School Education. Retrieved January 9, 2024, from https://oese.ed.gov/offices/office-state-grantee-relations-evidence-based-practices/state-and-grantee-relations/deadlines-and-announcements/

DeWitt Wallace-Reader's Digest Fund. (1997). *Recruiting, preparing and retaining teachers for America's schools. Progress report: Pathways to teaching careers*. https://wallacefoundation.org/sites/default/files/2023-06/Preparing-and-Retaining-Teachers.pdf

DiSchiano, Z. (2017, March 1). *Attracting and retaining teachers through creative, free perks*. HRX. https://www.tasb.org/services/hr-services/hrx/compensation-and-benefits/attracting-and-retaining-teachers-through-creative.aspx

District leaders' guide for developming a K–12 professional learning plan. (2023, April 5). Hanover Research. https://www.hanoverresearch.com/reports-and-briefs/district-leaders-guide-for-developing-a-k12-professional-learning-plan/?org=k-12-educationearning%20Plan

Dooley, K. (2022, August 29). *Using stay interviews to increase employee retention.* HRX. https://www.tasb.org/services/hr-services/hrx/hr-trends/stay-interviews-to-increase-retention.aspx

Dulin, M. (2022, April 25). *Pre-K enrollment in Texas is still behind prepandemic levels, which could widen educational disparities.* Rice University: Kinder Institute for Urban Research. https://kinder.rice.edu/urbanedge/pre-k-enrollment-texas-still-behind-prepandemic-levels-which-could-widen-educational

Dulin, M. (2023, February 15). *Public school enrollment is facing a 'demographic bubble.' Urban districts are already seeing its effects.* Rice University: Kinder Institute for Urban Research. https://kinder.rice.edu/urbanedge/public-school-enrollment-facing-demographic-bubble-urban-districts-are-already-seeing-its

Eastern Sierra Unified. (n.d.). EdSource. https://caaspp.edsource.org/sbac/eastern-sierra-unified-26736680000000

Educate Texas: Senate finance committee considers public and higher education budget. (2023, February 10). Communities Foundation of Texas. https://www.cftexas.org/news-events/blog/february-2023/senate-finance-committee-considers-budget

Education Code, Texas Stat. § 21.055 (1995, & rev. 2015). https://statutes.capitol.texas.gov/Docs/ED/htm/ED.21.htm

ESSER funding overview: ARP ESSER III spending plan as of December 2022. (2022). Spotslyvania County Public Schools. https://core-docs.s3.amazonaws.com/documents/asset/uploaded_file/2843/SCPS/2655057/SCPS_ARP_ESSER_III_Spending_Plan_-_Published_Dec_20_2022.pdf

ESSER III expenditure plan. (2021, June). Woodland Joint United School District. https://www.wjusd.org/documents/Departments/Ed%20Services/CARE/LCAP%20Webpage/22-23%20SY/2021_ESSER_III_Expenditure_Plan_Woodland_Joint_Unified_School_District_20220620.pdf

Finney, A. (2022, February 21). *'How dare you': Oakland school closure decision inspires new opposition efforts.* KQED. https://www.kqed.org/news/11905982/how-dare-you-oakland-school-closure-decision-inspires-new-opposition-efforts

Fresh Picks. (2022). *Pension fund expected to reach full funding ahead of schedule: Strong annual investment performance, legislative changes spur a growing fund.* Teacher Retirement System of Texas. https://www.trs.texas.gov/Pages/fresh-picks-202201-full-funding.aspx

Gartner, J., Becker, J., & Randazzo, A. (2022). *The next 10 years of Ed finance: Pension debt & reform.* Allovue. https://blog.allovue.com/10-for-10-pension-reform

Gates, S. M., Hamilton, L. S., Martorell, P., Burkhauser, S., Heaton, P., Pierson, A., Baird, M., Vuollo, M., Li, J. J., Lavery, D. C., Harvey, M., & Gu, K. (2014). *Preparing principals to raise student achievement: Implementation effects of the new leaders program in ten districts.* New Leaders, RAND Education, RAND Corporation. https://www.rand.org/pubs/research_reports/RR507.html

Gentz, S. (2022, August 25). *The final countdown: GEER edition.* Tech & Learning. https://www.techlearning.com/news/the-final-countdown-geer-edition

Gentz, S. (2023, June 16). *Was it too much too fast?* Digital Learning Collaborative. Retrieved December 27, 2023, from https://www.digitallearningcollab.com/blog/2022/4/7/was-it-too-much-too-fast

Gov. Reynolds launches new teacher and paraeducator registered apprenticeship. (2022, January 12). Iowa. https://governor.iowa.gov/press-release/2022-01-12/gov-reynolds-launches-new-teacher-and-paraeducator-registered

Governor of Virginia. (n.d.). *Our commitment to Virginia's children.* https://shorturl.at/hiYZ0

Gross, B. (2023, August 10). *Surging enrollment in virtual schools during the pandemics spurs new questions for policymakers.* CRPE. Retrieved December 27, 2023, from https://crpe.org/surging-enrollment-in-virtual-schools-during-the-pandemic-spurs-new-questions-for-policymakers/

Grow your own. (2023, November 1). Texas Education Agency. Retrieved December 28, 2023, from https://tea.texas.gov/texas-educators/educator-initiatives-and-performance/educator-initiatives/grow-your-own

Grow your own. (n.d.). Tennessee Department of Education. https://www.tn.gov/education/grow-your-own.html

Horn, M. B., & Tavenner, D. (Hosts). (2021, November 2). Where are students learning this year? (S3, E5) [Audio podcast episode]. In *Class Disrupted.* The74. https://www.the-74million.org/article/listen-class-disrupted-s3-e5-where-are-students-learning-this-year/

Jacobson, L. (2022, April 6). *'Those kids did not come back': Exclusive enrollment data shows students continue to flee urban districts as boom town schools and virtual academies thrive.* The74. https://www.the74million.org/article/covid-school-enrollment-students-move-away-from-urban-districts-virtual/

Jones, C. (2022, October 26). *Why some schools saw their scores soar despite COVID—and others didn't.* EdSource. https://edsource.org/2022/why-some-schools-saw-their-scores-soar-during-covid-and-others-didnt/680333

K–12 teaching and learning. (n.d.). Open Educational Resources Commons. https://oercommons.org/hubs/k12

Khalsa, S. A. (2017, Fall). *Succession planning: Getting it right.* National Association of Independent Schools. https://www.nais.org/magazine/independent-school/fall-2017/succession-planning-welcoming-a-new-head-of-school/

Khan, A. (2023, April). *How AI could save education* [Video]. TED. https://www.ted.com/talks/sal_khan_how_ai_could_save_not_destroy_education

Killion, J. (2013). *Professional learning plans: A workbook for states, districts, and schools.* Learning Forward. https://learningforward.org/wp-content/uploads/2017/09/professional-learning-plans.pdf

Klein, A. (2020, November 29). *New jobs bill offers $23 billion for education.* EducationWeek. Retrieved December 29, 2023, from https://www.edweek.org/policy-politics/new-jobs-bill-offers-23-billion-for-education/2009/12

Koruth, M. A. (2022, June 6). *Teacher shortages continue. Here's what New Jersey is doing to make it easier to hire more.* NorthJersey. https://www.northjersey.com/story/news/2022/06/06/nj-teacher-shortages-being-addressed-but-additional-action-needed/7500731001/

Lost Hills Union Elementary. (n.d.). EdSource. https://caaspp.edsource.org/sbac/lost-hills-union-elementary-15635940000000

McNeel, B. (2022, September 29). *In West Texas, Fort Stockton's solution to a teacher shortage is a motel*. The Texas Tribune. https://www.texastribune.org/2022/09/29/texas-teachers-shortage-fort-stockton-motel/

Mountain Valley Unified. (n.d.). EdSource. https://caaspp.edsource.org/sbac/mountain-valley-unified-53750280000000?_gl=1*1h2chyx*_ga*NTc3NjA3NzY1LjE2NzgxMzIxNzU.*_ga_475QR6J62K*MTY3ODEzMjE3Ni4xLjAuMTY3ODEzMjE3Ni42MC4wLjA

O'Donoghue, J. (2023, June 9). *Louisiana lawmakers pass state budget plan with only temporary teacher pay increase*. Louisiana Illuminator. Retrieved December 28, 2023, from https://lailluminator.com/2023/06/08/louisiana-lawmakers-pass-state-budget-plan-with-only-temporary-teacher-pay-increase/

Oxford English Dictionary. (2006). Augmented reality. In *Oxford English dictionary*. Retrieved December 28, 2023, from https://www.oed.com/dictionary/augmented-reality_n?tab=factsheet#9933893672

Oxford English Dictionary. (2023a). Artificial intelligence. In *Oxford English dictionary*. Retrieved December 28, 2023, from https://www.oed.com/dictionary/artificial-intelligence_n?tab=meaning_and_use#38531565

Oxford English Dictionary. (2023b). Interacted. In *Oxford English dictionary*. Retrieved December 29, 2023, from https://www.oed.com/dictionary/interact_v?tab=factsheet#239541

Oxford English Dictionary. (2023c). Superimpose. In *Oxford English dictionary*. Retrieved December 29, 2023, from https://www.oed.com/dictionary/superimpose_v?tab=factsheet#19671827

Oxford English Dictionary. (2023d). Three-dimensional. In *Oxford English dictionary*. Retrieved December 29, 2023, from https://www.oed.com/dictionary/three-dimensional_adj-a?tab=factsheet#9918643517

Oxford English Dictionary. (2023e). Virtual reality. In *Oxford English dictionary*. Retrieved December 28, 2023, from https://www.oed.com/dictionary/virtual-reality_n?tab=factsheet#15654690

Parents' school preferences [Figure on homepage]. (2023, December 18). EdChoice. Retrieved January 9, 2024, from https://www.edchoice.org/

Performance assessment of competency education. (n.d.). New Hampshire Department of Education. https://www.education.nh.gov/who-we-are/division-of-learner-support/bureau-of-instructional-support/performance-assessment-for-competency-education

Plato. (2013). *Phaedrus* (B. Jowett, Trans.). Project Gutenberg. Original work published in 370 B.C. https://www.gutenberg.org/files/1636/1636-h/1636-h.htm

Professional learning plan. (2022, August). Clear Creek Independent School District. https://resources.finalsite.net/images/v1661263472/ccisdnet/xez9lyewly8jgmrhuiey/DMAREG_ProfessionalLearningPlan_07-18-22.pdf

Randazzo, A., & Moody, J. (2023, March). *Hidden education funding cuts: How growing teacher pension debt stresses America's K–12 education budgets*. Equable Institute. https://equable.org/hidden-funding-cuts/

Rhodes, A., & Szabo, J. (2023, May 19). *Parents tend to choose schools based on their own educational experience.* The74. https://www.the74million.org/article/parents-tend-to-choose-schools-based-on-their-own-educational-experience/?utm_source=The+74+Million+Newsletter&utm_campaign=bf69d41933-EMAIL_CAMPAIGN_2022_07_27_07_47_COPY_01&utm_medium=email&utm_term=0_077b986842-bf69d41933-176993516

Roche, D. (2023, March 20). *Burbio school tracker 3/20: Changes in Virginia.* Burbio. https://about.burbio.com/weekly-updates/burbio-school-tracker-3/20-changes-in-virginia

Roza, M., Aldeman, C., & Silberstein, K. (2022, August 18). *30-min webinar: The financial forecast is in! School district budgets are headed for a wild ride.* Edunomics Lab: The Study of Education Finance. https://edunomicslab.org/2022/08/18/financial-forecast-webinar/

Santos, D. (2022, December 13). *Cross-curricular activities: how to create meaningful learning opportunities?* Cambridge. Retrieved December 30, 2023, from https://www.cambridge.org/elt/blog/2022/12/07/cross-curricular-activities-how-create-meaningful-learning-opportunities/

Sawchuck, S. (2022, July 28). *Better pay would keep teachers from quitting. But there's more to it.* EducationWeek. Retrieved December 29, 2023, from https://www.edweek.org/teaching-learning/better-pay-would-keep-teachers-from-quitting-but-theres-more-to-it/2022/07

Schladen, M. (2023, March 16). *Ohio state teachers retirement system had massive investment in failed bank.* The74. https://www.the74million.org/article/ohio-state-teachers-retirement-system-had-massive-investment-in-failed-bank/?utm_source=substack&utm_medium=email

Schmid, H. (2022, June 6). *Longer public schools closed for pandemic, more students they lost.* Illinois Policy. Retrieved December 28, 2023, from https://www.illinoispolicy.org/longer-public-schools-closed-for-pandemic-more-students-they-lost/

Schneiderman, M. (2022). *How the pandemic has (re)shaped K–12 teacher professional learning: Survey findings, research brief and recommendations.* D2L. https://www.d2l.com/resources/assets/ways-to-support-teachers-professional-development/?asset=7015W0000009bpSQAQ

School district teaching permits. (n.d.). Texas Education Agency. https://tea.texas.gov/texas-educators/certification/school-district-teaching-permits#:~:text=Since%201995%2C%20Texas%20law%20has,for%20Educator%20Certification%20(SBEC)

Schools worth visiting. (2023, December 5). Getting Smart. Retrieved December 29, 2023, from https://www.gettingsmart.com/schools-worth-visiting/

Schwalbach, J. (2023, May 23). *School districts often oppose open enrollment. Why that's a mistake.* The74. https://www.the74million.org/article/school-districts-often-oppose-open-enrollment-why-thats-a-mistake/?utm_source=The%2074%20Million%20Newsletter&utm_campaign=991791c0d7-EMAIL_CAMPAIGN_2022_07_27_07_47_COPY_01&utm_medium=email&utm_term=0_077b986842-991791c0d7-176993516

Schwartz, S. (2023, March 8). *Building the superintendent pipeline: Advice from 3 district leaders.* EducationWeek. https://www.edweek.org/leadership/building-the-superintendent-pipeline-advice-from-3-district-leaders/2023/03

Sierra, A. (2023, April 17). *An Eastern Oregon district does the math and finds way to give teachers 'life changing' raises.* OPB.

https://www.opb.org/article/2023/04/17/baker-county-oregon-teacher-salary-bump-legisture-debate/

Stay interview sample questionnaire. (n.d.). HelpSide. https://www.helpside.com/wp-content/uploads/2017/12/Stay-Interview.pdf

Stone, C. (2020, April 16). *Fiscal stimulus needed to fight recessions.* Center on Budget and Policy Priorities. https://www.cbpp.org/research/fiscal-stimulus-needed-to-fight-recessions

Sturgis, C. (2020, February 5). *Highland tech charter school—putting it all together.* Aurora Institute. Retrieved December 28, 2023, from https://aurora-institute.org/cw_post/highland-tech-charter-school-putting-it-all-together/

Succession planning (with free template downloads). (n.d.). Indeed. https://www.indeed.com/hire/c/info/succession-planning-template#3

Tamez-Robledo, N. (2022, June 22). *Can four-day school weeks keep teachers from leaving?* EdSurge. https://www.edsurge.com/news/2022-06-22-can-four-day-school-weeks-keep-teachers-from-leaving

TDOE awards $4.5 million grow your own grants to create pathways to become a teacher for free. (2023, March 4). Tennessee Department of Education. Retrieved December 28, 2023, from https://www.tn.gov/education/news/2021/6/23/tdoe-awards--4-5-million-grow-your-own-grants-to-create-pathways-to-become-a-teacher-for-free-.html

Texas Education Agency. (2021, September 16). *Build your own tutoring system.* Retrieved December 28, 2023, from https://tea.texas.gov/texas-schools/health-safety-discipline/covid/build-your-own-tutoring-system

Timeline of the elementary and secondary school emergency relief funds (ESSER). (2021, May 24). Afterschool Alliance. https://www.afterschoolalliance.org/documents/Funding-Timeline_final.pdf

Timmons, J., Tate, C., & Jiminez, L. (n.d.). *Liquidation extension requests for CARES-ESSER and CARES-GEER.* Office of State and Grantee Relations, U.S. Department of Education. https://oese.ed.gov/files/2022/10/WEBINAR-10.3.22_Liquidation-Extension-for-CARES-ESSER-and-CARES-GEER.pdf

Trope, P., Milanowski, A., Garrison-Mogren, R., Webber, A., Gutmann, B., Reisner, E., Goertz, M., & Bachman, M. (2015, September). *State, district, and school implementation of reforms promoted under the Recovery Act: 2009–10 through 2011–12. The final report from charting the progress of education reform: An evaluation of the Recovery Act's role* (NCEE 2-15-4016). National Center for Education Evaluation and Regional Assistance, Institute of Education Sciences, U.S. Department of Education. https://ies.ed.gov/ncee/pubs/20154016/pdf/20154016.pdf

Tufekci, Z. (2022, December 15). *What would Plato say about ChatGPT?* New York Times. https://www.nytimes.com/2022/12/15/opinion/chatgpt-education-ai-technology.html

Updated ESSER III spending plan. (2022, December 20). Accomack County Public Schools. https://www.accomack.k12.va.us/ourpages/auto/2015/5/16/46929527/Updated%20ESSER%20III%20Spending%20Plan.pdf?rnd=1672410657473

Ventsias, T. (2021, August 17). *People recall information better through virtual reality, says new UMD study*. University of Maryland. Retrieved on December 28, 2023, from https://

umdrightnow.umd.edu/people-recall-information-better-through-virtual-reality-says-new-umd-study

Waite, C. (2023, May 22). *Teachers want to innovate. Schools that don't let them are losing out.* The 74. https://www.the74million.org/article/teachers-want-to-innovate-schools-that-dont-let-them-are-losing-out/?utm_source=The%2074%20Million%20Newsletter&utm_campaign=bf69d41933-EMAIL_CAMPAIGN_2022_07_27_07_47_COPY_01&utm_medium=email&utm_term=0_077b986842-bf69d41933-176993516

Walker, T. (2022, February 1). *Survey: Alarming number of educators may soon leave the profession.* neaToday. https://www.nea.org/nea-today/all-news-articles/survey-alarming-number-educators-may-soon-leave-profession

Warren, J. (2023, February 8). *Senate finance committee—enrollment trends* [Video]. Vimeo. https://vimeo.com/797038043

Watson, J. (2023, January 26). *Will AI transform education? The case for.* Digital Learning Collaborative. https://www.digitallearningcollab.com/blog/2023/1/26/will-ai-transform-education-the-case-for

Watson, J. (2023, May 18). *Elearning days are more like emergency remote learning than like online learning.* Digital Learning Collaborative. https://www.digitallearningcollab.com/blog/2023/5/18/elearning-days-are-more-like-emergency-remote-learning-than-like-online-learning

Will, M. (2021, June 4). *4 ways districts are giving teachers more flexibility in their jobs.* EducationWeek. Retrieved December 29, 2023, from https://www.edweek.org/teaching-learning/4-ways-districts-are-giving-teachers-more-flexibility-in-their-jobs/2021/05

Will, M. (2022, June 30). *States relax teacher certification rules to combat shortages.* EducationWeek. Retrieved December 28, 2023, from https://www.edweek.org/teaching-learning/states-relax-teacher-certification-rules-to-combat-shortages/2022/06

Will, M. (2023, July 11). *The interstate teacher mobility compact is now in effect. Here's what that means.* EducationWeek. Retrieved December 28, 2023, from https://www.edweek.org/teaching-learning/the-interstate-teacher-mobility-compact-is-now-in-effect-heres-what-that-means/2023/07?utm_source=li&utm_medium=soc&utm_campaign=edi

Will, M. (2023, May 31). *How these state and district leaders are solving teacher shortages.* EducationWeek. Retrieved December 28, 2023, from https://www.edweek.org/leadership/how-these-state-and-district-leaders-are-solving-teacher-shortages/2023/05

Windes, I. (2023, May 1). *How San Antonio ISD is paying for its largest teacher pay raise in years.* The Texas Tribune. https://www.texastribune.org/2023/05/01/san-antonio-isd-teacher-pay-raise/

Woodbridge, L. (2019, March 18). *It's not a game.* SmartBrief. https://corp.smartbrief.com/original/2019/03/its-not-game

Made in the USA
Monee, IL
29 February 2024